ginia Woolf Beryl Bainbridge *Simone de Beauvoir* Hilaire Belloc Jeffrey Bernard **Caroline Blackwood** Quent

isp R.B. Cunninghame Graham Charles Doughty Roland Firbank **John** ... im Gor

I. Lawrence ***W.Heath Robinson*** Oliver Sacks Edith Sitwell Tom Hedley ... *Simone*

uvoir Hilaire Belloc Jeffrey Bernard **Caroline Blackwood** Quenti ... Graha

arles Doughty Roland Firbank **John Galsworthy** Elinor Glyn Edith Sitwe ... ***W.Hea***

binson Oliver Sacks Tom Hedley Virginia Woolf Beryl Bainbridge *Si* ... c Jeffr

rnard **Caroline Blackwood** Quentin Crisp R.B. Cunninghame Graham Charles Doughty Roland Firba

n **Galsworthy** Elinor Glyn Maxim Gorky D.H. Lawrence ***W.Heath Robinson*** Oliver Sacks Edith Sitwell To

dley Virginia Woolf Beryl Bainbridge *Simone de Beauvoir* Hilaire Belloc Jeffrey Bernard **Caroline Blackwo**

entin Crisp R.B. Cunninghame Graham Charles Doughty Roland Firbank **John Galsworthy** Elinor Gl

xim Gorky D.H. Lawrence ***W.Heath Robinson*** Oliver Sacks Tom HedleyVirginia Woolf Beryl Bainbridge *Simo*

Beauvoir Edith Sitwell Hilaire Belloc Jeffrey Bernard **Caroline Blackwood** Quentin Crisp R.B. Cunninghan

aham Charles Doughty Roland Firbank **John Galsworthy** Elinor Glyn Maxim Gorky D.H. Lawrence ***W.Hea***

binson Oliver Sacks Edith Sitwell Tom Hedley Virginia Woolf Beryl Bainbridge *Simone de Beauvoir* Hilaire Bell

frey Bernard **Caroline Blackwood** Quentin Crisp R.B. Cunninghame Graham Charles Doughty Rola

bank **John Galsworthy** Elinor Glyn Maxim Gorky D.H. Lawrence ***W.Heath Robinson*** Oliver Sacks Edith Sitw

n Hedley Virginia Woolf Beryl Bainbridge *Simone de Beauvoir* Hilaire Belloc Jeffrey Bernard **Caroline Blackwo**

entin Crisp R.B. Cunninghame Graham Charles Doughty Roland Firbank **John Galsworthy** Elinor Gl

xim Gorky D.H. Lawrence ***W.Heath Robinson*** Oliver Sacks Edith Sitwell Tom Hedley Virginia Woolf Be

nbridge *Simone de Beauvoir* Hilaire Belloc Jeffrey Bernard **Caroline Blackwood** Quentin Crisp R.

nninghame Graham Charles Doughty Roland Firbank **John Galsworthy** Elinor Glyn Maxim Gorky D.

wrence ***W.Heath Robinson*** Oliver Sacks Edith Sitwell Tom Hedley Virginia Woolf Beryl Bainbridge *Simone*

uvoir Hilaire Belloc Jeffrey Bernard **Caroline Blackwood** Quentin Crisp R.B. Cunninghame Graha

arles Doughty Roland Firbank **John Galsworthy** Elinor Glyn Maxim Gorky D.H. Lawrence ***W.Heath Robins***

ver Sacks Edith Sitwell Tom Hedley Virginia Woolf Jeffrey Bernard Beryl Bainbridge *Simone de Beauvoir* Hila

loc Jeffrey Bernard **Caroline Blackwood** Quentin Crisp R.B. Hilaire Belloc Jeffrey Bernard **Caroli**

ckwood Roland Firbank Quentin Crisp Edith Sitwell R.B. Cunninghame Graham Charls Sacks Hilaire Bell

Heath Robinson Cunninghame Graham Charles Doughty Oliver Sacks Edith Sitwell Tom Hedley Roland Firba

WOOLF AT
THE DOOR

Duckworth: 100 Years of Bloomsbury Behaviour

Gerald Duckworth, founder of the firm.

WOOLF AT THE DOOR

Duckworth: 100 Years of Bloomsbury Behaviour

JOHN JOLLIFFE

Duckworth

First published in 1998 by
Gerald Duckworth & Co. Ltd.
61 Frith Street, London W1V 5TA

Designed by Sebastian Conran Associates

A catalogue record for this book is available from the British Library.

ISBN 0 7156 2856 9

Picture credits
(numbers refer to the pages of this book)

Tate Gallery Archives *6, 7*; National Portrait Gallery *12, 15, 18, 20, 31, 44, 49*; Christopher Davson *20*; Anthony Duckworth-Chad *24*; Dom Philip Jebb *27*; Sheffield City Art Galleries & Bridgeman Art Library, copyright Annabel Cole *36*; Violet Powell *39* (Anthony Powell & Tom Balston); Mervyn Horder *52*; Hulton Getty *63*; Solo Syndication Ltd *68*; Bridgeman Art Library *70*; BFI Stills, Posters and Designs *72*; Sally Soames/Times Newspapers Ltd *77*; Jerry Bauer *84*; Lucinda Rogers *98*

Printed in Great Britain by
The Bath Press

CONTENTS

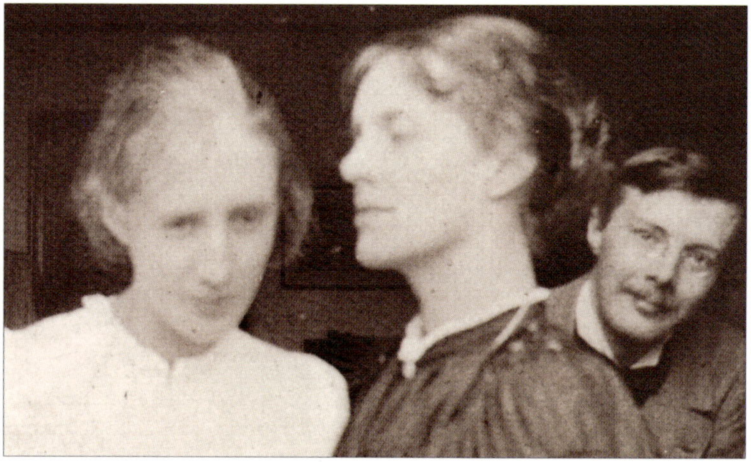

Above: Virginia Stephen (later Woolf) with Gerald and Stella Duckworth, 1896.

Right: Gerald at Virginia's feet, 1897.

ARISE, SIR DUCKWORTH!

As a child of seven, Gerald Duckworth's half-sister Virginia Woolf began to compose a history of the Duckworth family. The only surviving fragment runs as follows:

'One day when William Rufus was hunting in the New Forest he shot a duck. It fell into the middle of a pond and could not be recovered; but an active little page boy waded out into the water and recovered the bird. The King drew his sword and dubbed the lad, saying "Arise, Sir Duckworth! For surely thou art worth many ducks." '

HORACE
A Life
PETER LEVI

NANSEN
ROLAND HUNTFORD

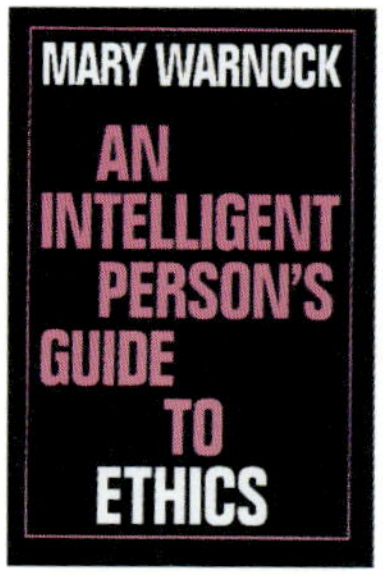
MARY WARNOCK
AN INTELLIGENT PERSON'S GUIDE TO ETHICS

Nicholas Hammond
THE GENIUS OF ALEXANDER THE GREAT

Roman Aqueducts & Water Supply
A. Trevor Hodge

LEARN ANCIENT GREEK
PETER JONES

BRUNO BETTELHEIM
THE OTHER SIDE OF MADNESS
NINA SUTTON

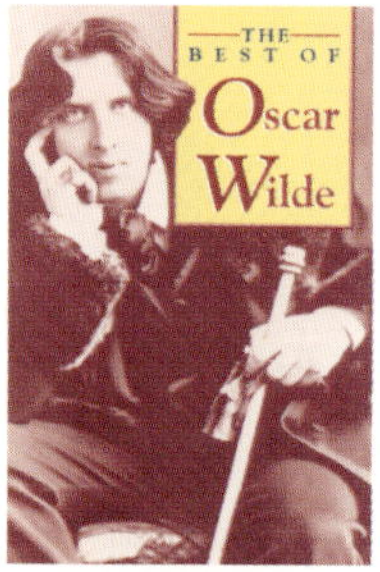
THE BEST OF Oscar Wilde

BERYL BAINBRIDGE
Every Man for Himself

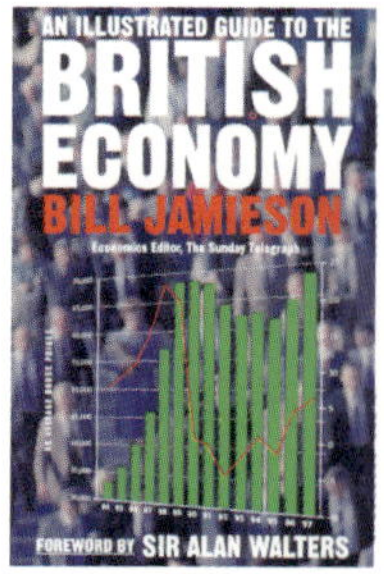
AN ILLUSTRATED GUIDE TO THE BRITISH ECONOMY
BILL JAMIESON
FOREWORD BY SIR ALAN WALTERS

ROGER SCRUTON
AN INTELLIGENT PERSON'S GUIDE TO PHILOSOPHY

ALEXANDER OF APHRODISIAS
Ethical Problems
Translated by R.W. Sharples
Ancient Commentators on Aristotle

ARCHAEOLOGY EXPLAINED
Keith Branigan

The Sayings of
JANE
AUSTEN

James Longrigg
GREEK MEDICINE
From the Heroic to the Hellenistic Age
A SOURCE BOOK

THE SPEECHES OF CICERO
Paul MacKendrick

A.L. ROWSE
HISTORIANS I have known

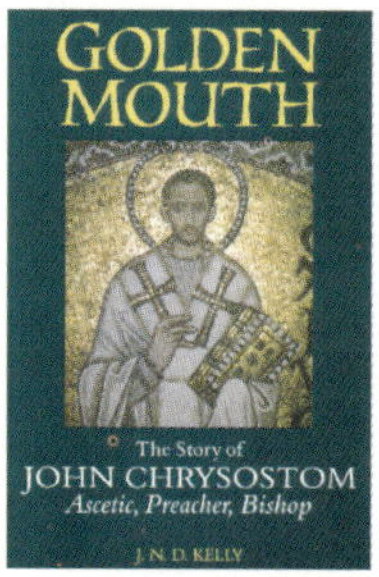
GOLDEN MOUTH
The Story of
JOHN CHRYSOSTOM
Ascetic, Preacher, Bishop
J. N. D. KELLY

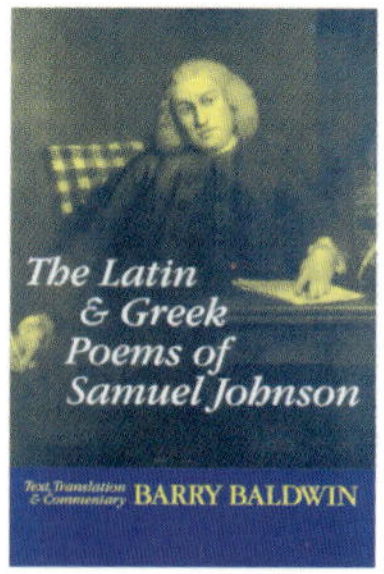
The Latin & Greek Poems of Samuel Johnson
BARRY BALDWIN

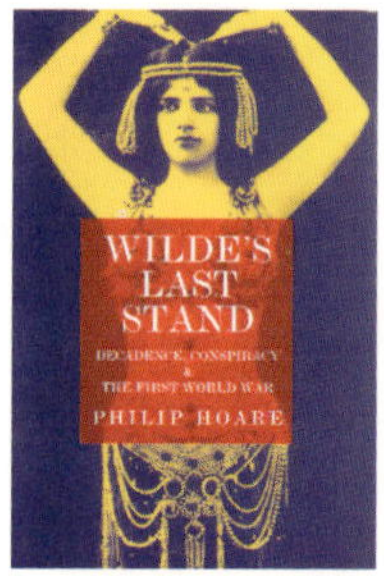
WILDE'S LAST STAND
PHILIP HOARE

LIST OF ILLUSTRATIONS

When I was taken on as a graduate trainee at Longmans in 1959, nobody in their right mind would have predicted that within thirty-five years nearly all the then great names in British publishing would have been swallowed up by foreign or corporate buyers, and ceased to operate independently: Longmans themselves, Collins, Macmillan, Cape, Chatto & Windus, Bodley Head, Hutchinson, Eyre & Spottiswoode, Allen & Unwin, Rupert Hart-Davis, and many other lesser lights. John Murray and Faber are perhaps the outstanding exceptions to this tendency, and Duckworth, which seemed in those days to be a down-at-heel, unadventurous, frowsty sort of firm, probably on its last legs, has now reached its centenary in a healthy financial position, a state of affairs till then unthinkable. Many of the hares in the great publishing race have run out of steam, but Duckworth, the obscure tortoise, is alive and forging ahead.

The story of how this has come about is a remarkable one; plenty of ups and downs, with the latter prevailing. There have been dramas, scandals, even a lock-out, but the story ends, almost miraculously, with a great recovery from the brink of total disaster. The task of composing it has been if not perhaps hindered, then certainly shortened, by the destruction of most of the firm's early records in a fire in the office in 1935. It is worth mentioning here that the records of board meetings in the company minute book, which survived the fire and remained in use for several decades, are generally of the sketchiest and most unrevealing kind, and were often written up many months after the event. Fortunately, much pioneering work on the surviving material was done by Mervyn (Lord) Horder, who joined the firm in 1938, and was chairman for twenty-five years after the war. His brief account of the first fifty years of the firm's existence is invaluable, and I am grateful for the information that he gave me before his unexpected death in 1997, which unhappily prevented me from consulting him about the more recent past.

I am also grateful to Mrs Henry Duckworth, the widow of Gerald Duckworth's nephew, who kindly provided the photograph of Gerald, and some other information, and to Mr Anthony Duckworth-Chad for the Gerald's wedding photograph. I am greatly indebted to Mr Anthony Powell, and Heinemann Publishers, for permission to quote from his book of memoirs *Messengers of Day*, which is an almost unique source of information about life in Duckworth's office between 1926 and 1934; and also from his novel *What's Become of Waring?*, which he wrote soon after that time, and which is highly relevant to the firm's history. I am also grateful to his wife, Lady Violet Powell, for help in tracing photographs, and to her sister Lady Pansy Lamb, whose novel *August* was published by the firm in 1931, and who is now the senior surviving Duckworth author. Next, I would like to thank Mrs Patrick Crichton-Stuart for her kind hospitality, and for information about the period when her husband was director of Duckworth.

Turning to more recent times, Colin Haycraft's widow Anna has been extremely helpful in a variety of ways, and I am deeply grateful for her kind hospitality both in London and Wales. Lord Smith helped by giving me the Joseph Rowntree Reform Trust's point of view about the disagreements that arose, at a painful time, between the Trust and the executive directors of Duckworth. Lady Quinton, one of the most distinguished and stimulating of contemporary sculptors, kindly gave me a vivid description of working with Sir Hugh Lloyd-Jones on three books for Duckworth. I am indebted to Jasper Griffin, Public Orator at the University of Oxford, for his translations of the Latin and Greek couplets composed by Colin Haycraft. Professor Richard Gregory also gave me details of his recollections of working with Colin Haycraft on books of great distinction, and Beryl Bainbridge has been endlessly helpful in conveying something of the flavour of the unique Duckworth atmosphere.

I would also like to thank the present directors of Duckworth for the help they have been able to give me in describing the most recent part of the story of an often eccentric and accident-prone firm, which under its present leadership now seems set for a period of well organised success on a scale which it has never enjoyed before; in particular I thank Deborah Blake for details which would not have been available otherwise, and for much editorial help.

Finally, I would like to salute Stephen Hill, without whom Duckworth would never have risen again, and to thank him most warmly for all his encouragement and for the generous facilities which he provided.

THE LETHARGIC ALLIGATOR
1898-1918

Gerald de l'Etang Duckworth was born in 1871, six weeks after the sudden death of his father at the age of forty-four. Records of the Duckworth family go back to the time of the dissolution of the monasteries, and in 1538 they had become established as landowners at Musbury, near Bury in Lancashire. Many of the later Duckworths were lawyers, without reaching the heights of their profession, but maintaining their local position.

In 1855 William Duckworth ventured south and acquired the attractive property of Orchardleigh Park, near Frome, in Somerset, and it was from there, forty years later, that his granddaughter Margaret, who was Gerald's first cousin, married Henry Newbolt, later to become an immensely popular poet, famous for his lines beginning 'There's a deathless hush in the Close tonight', and ending with the refrain, 'Play up! play up! and play the game!' However, this was not a significant link between the Duckworths and the world of letters, and although in due course Gerald was to publish a generous amount of poetry there is no record of his ever having tried to secure Newbolt for his list.

In March 1877 Gerald Duckworth's mother Julia remarried. Her new husband, Leslie Stephen, was an accomplished and attractive man of letters, later knighted. Much light is thrown on the family background both before and after this time, by an account that he wrote after Julia's death in 1895 for the benefit of his second family, later known as Vanessa Bell, Adrian Stephen and Virginia Woolf. Vanessa was born in 1879 and was therefore eight years younger than Gerald; Virginia three years later in 1882. Their father's account was probably only written for family consumption, as an outlet for the emotional intensity which was one of its author's chief characteristics. But mercifully for those interested in this background, it was admirably edited by Alan Bell, the present Librarian at the London Library, and published by the Oxford University Press in 1977, under the title by which it was known in the family, Sir Leslie Stephen's *Mausoleum Book*. It contains much material invaluable for the understanding of the family, but not strictly relevant to the history of Duckworth.

But to give some idea of the eminence of Gerald's stepfather in the literary world, he had been the first editor of the *Dictionary of National Biography*, resigning the post in 1891 but remaining a major contributor. He had also edited the influential and high-calibre *Cornhill Magazine* for ten years, been President of the London Library, and contributed the volumes on Pope, Swift, George Eliot and Hobbes to a series of books on English Men of Letters. Like other numbers of his intellectually illustrious family, he more than once suffered breakdowns from overwork and was also hit very hard by the loss of two wives, to both of whom he was deeply devoted. Though Gerald never

Virginia Woolf by Vanessa Bell, 1912.

attained his stepfather's intellectual eminence, it is not hard to see why he chose the profession that he did.

The *Mausoleum Book* contains a number of references to Gerald. He is described as 'delicate as was to be expected from the circumstances of his birth, and his health caused occasional anxiety. When he was six it was thought that it could be improved by a visit to Australia, but this was later considered unnecessary.' But tragedy struck the family again in 1895 when Julia Stephen died, and the burden of supporting their father in his immense distress fell heavily on the shoulders of Vanessa and Virginia, the youngest child, who certainly suffered greatly from it. In 1901, three years after the foundation of the firm, Sir Leslie records severely that 'Gerald has been to Aix les Bains for rheumatism. I wish he were more attentive to sanitary conditions of life.' Two similar visits are recorded in the next four months, but Sir Leslie himself fell ill again and died in February 1904, at which point the *Mausoleum Book* ends.

In spite of his connection with the Stephens, Gerald himself was not particularly interested in books or reading, but as in many other cases, this did not prevent him from laying the foundations of what was to become a distinctly successful firm, though one which was to be bedevilled with financial problems as a result of under-capitalisation, as will be seen. He was joined at the start by A.R. Waller, an older colleague from the firm of J.M. Dent, a leading publisher where Gerald had served an apprenticeship. Waller left after three years to become Secretary to the Syndics of the Cambridge University Press, where he remained until his death in 1922. He probably played a part in supplying the literary element that was largely lacking in Gerald's nature. He was what used to be called a great bookman, edited the works of Abraham Cowley, Crashaw and Matthew Prior, and also (jointly with Arnold Glover) of Hazlitt. His name, or rather half of it, survived sandwiched in the middle of what remained the firm's bizarre and now obsolete address for telegrams, GERWALDUCK; though in view of Gerald's middle name, and of Virginia's childhood fantasy, DUCKPOND would have been a less clumsy and more euphonious formula.

In all probability, the foundation of numerous publishing companies in the second half of the nineteenth century owed much to the general intellectual ferment which bubbled and frothed in England round the ideas of Darwin, Huxley and Richard Owen in science, Newman and the Oxford Movement in matters of religion, and perhaps to a lesser extent to historians of the ancient world like Grote and Grundy, and those of modern times such as Macaulay and Froude. In fiction, Thackeray, Dickens and Trollope had all caused their readers to buy the magazines where the novels first appeared, and sent them hurrying to the popular libraries when they appeared in volume form. But much less of this would have happened without Forster's Education Act of 1870, England being far behind Europe, and even further behind Scotland in this respect.

Forster, who was a Quaker, was vice-president of the Privy Council's committee for education in Gladstone's ministry, which aimed at ending the rivalry between church and chapel schools that had operated since they first began to receive government grants in 1833. Further education acts in 1876 and 1880 had made school compulsory for children under ten, and this was made free in 1891. Most of these

R.B. Cunninghame Graham by T.B. Wirgman, 1918.

measures came in under Liberal ministries, but in 1902, not long after Gerald Duckworth had put up his brass plate in Henrietta Street, Balfour's Unionist government carried yet another Education Act which simplified the administrative muddle by setting up local education authorities. Public money was made available to ensure standards of teaching and to build the new grammar schools which were to become such an advance on most of what had gone before. Secondary as well as elementary education was now in place, and in that television-free age, the market for books grew and grew.

There is no evidence that Gerald Duckworth was in any way inspired by the spirit of enlightenment which had gathered strength and achieved so much. What appears to have motivated him were the less exalted pleasures of the theatre and the ballroom, and all the extensive though formal offerings of the London season, followed by a course of recuperation at Droitwich Spa.

After a few years of work with Dent, Gerald launched out with his own imprint in 1898. Partly thanks to Waller, the firm's lists in its first few years contained a number of books which were still in demand fifty years later, when Mervyn Horder, one of the firm's then directors, composed a brief account of its first half-century. Far more important however than Waller was the part played from 1901 to 1920 by Duckworth's literary adviser and reader, Edward Garnett. Horder states that it was Garnett's discernment, enthusiasm and sincerity, together with his unlimited editorial patience, that was responsible for the firm's early and considerable success. He brought to the list famous authors as diverse as Maxim Gorky, W.H. Hudson, Charles

Doughty and D.H. Lawrence, and also a dashing Scotsman, R.B. Cunninghame Graham, a close friend of both Hudson and Joseph Conrad, whom he helped with *Nostromo.*

Cunninghame Graham is now almost entirely forgotten, but deserves to be remembered far more than many who are. He had eight books published by Duckworth between 1902 and 1916, and has a good claim to be described first among those who put the new firm on the literary map. By birth he was an exceptionally forceful and violently outspoken Stirlingshire laird, descended from the Graham who murdered James I of Scotland in 1447. But his Spanish grandmother was perhaps an even stronger formative influence, and he was to spend many months as a cattle rancher and horse dealer in wild and remote areas of South America, and liked to be known to his intimates as Don Roberto. He was to become one of the most brilliant and paradoxical characters of his day and his portraits indicate that he was well aware of his talents. At home, he was a fearless and even violent champion of the poor and oppressed, and was quite capable of staring out Gladstone, whom he greatly disliked. He sat in Parliament, as the first real socialist to do so, but nominally as a Liberal, from 1885 to 1892, at the height of the Home Rule crisis, and regularly arrived at Westminster on his equally fiery Argentine mustang, 'Pampa'. In 1887 he took part in a savagely mishandled meeting of protest, later known as the Battle of Trafalgar Square, against the imprisonment of an Irish MP, William O'Brien. He was himself imprisoned for four weeks on a doubtful charge, in spite of being defended in court by the subsequent Prime Minister, H.H. Asquith. Later he became founder and president of the first Labour Party, and was also eventually elected President of the Scottish National Party. He was easily the most flamboyant figure ever to appear on the Duckworth list, but his literary skill did not really match his general panache and his self-important desire to describe his romantic experiences. He was however an exceptional horseman, performing what amounted to circus tricks on Pampa in Rotten Row, and when the war came he was sent by the government to Uruguay to buy horses for the British Army.

Later, he was Bernard Shaw's model in *Captain Brassbound's Conversion,* and also for Saranoff in *Arms and the Man.* He returned the compliment by commenting on *Saint Joan*: 'I never thought to see a simple, beautiful story so vulgarised and made common ... Shaw is a clever, kind and most charitable man, who has written some exquisitely funny things, but Tragedy is not for him ... Shaw, to my mind, saw (and felt) nothing, and out of the most beautiful story, he made a cultured Irish Protestant farce. It is his damned suburban *culture* I kick at.'

Whatever the real merits of Cunninghame Graham's work, his personality gained him many admirers. His friend Wilfrid Blunt said that he 'saw in him the only competitor to beat Kipling on his own ground', while Hudson, who dedicated *El Ombu* to him, told him that 'your writing is more refreshing and stimulating to my soul than that of any other living author'. In 1914, he was again in trouble for breaking windows in Pall Mall in support of a dock strike, and served another brief spell in prison. After 1918 he published a further eight books with Heinemann, and it may have been that after the departure of Garnett from Duckworth, the vast temperamental gulf between him and Gerald accounted for his move to another list. To compare him with later figures, he was a kind of mixture between Julian Grenfell and Tam Dalyell, with a strong flavour of Don Quixote thrown in. His books are very hard to come by today, but his Scottish and South American stories could well be reprinted.

In 1904 the team of Duckworth, Garnett and Milsted (who had replaced Waller) was joined by another name to remain famous in publishing for most of the rest of the century, Jonathan Cape. He began as the London sales representative, became 'manager' in 1909, and was in chief control of the firm for the first two years of the war. Gerald was however unwilling to make him a director, allegedly for snobbish reasons, and in 1920 Cape left to found his own firm, and succeeded in taking Garnett with him by the simple method of offering him more money than Duckworth was willing to pay. This is the first of many examples of Duckworth losing advantages through a financial inability to retain them. With much help from Garnett, Cape was to publish, with great success, many famous authors who would otherwise have been Duckworth's.

The books fell into no real pattern. Leslie Stephen's own Ford Lectures on *English Literature and Society in the 18th Century* found themselves (posthumously) next to Professor John Percival's massive textbook, *Agricultural Botany*, and also Strindberg's play *The Father*, early evidence of Gerald's keen interest in the theatre. Leslie Stephen had in fact earlier written to a friend that Gerald's partner 'has, I hear, an objection to Agnostic publications; so that I shall not ruin them by inflicting my works on the firm'. The Ford Lectures, however, must have passed the test.

There were also two unsuccessful novels by Galsworthy on the list, written under the improbable pen-name of John Sinjohn. It was often wrongly rumoured that Duckworth turned down what was to become the *Forsyte Saga*. What in fact happened was that after these first two failures, Gerald advised Galsworthy to take his next novel to Heinemann, and instead to sit down and write a play for Duckworth. His third novel, and fourth, were equally unsuccessful, but Heinemann persevered, and was eventually well rewarded. Duckworth however went on to publish Galsworthy's plays, twenty-seven in all, beginning with *The Silver Box* in 1904, and ending with *The Roof* in 1928. And in 1929, copying Hodder & Stoughton who had done the same for Barrie the year before, Duckworth published an omnibus edition of *The Plays of John Galsworthy*, of 1,158 pages, at 8/6 net. Galsworthy himself was certain that the huge first printing of 40,000 was far in excess of what could be sold, but within three months a further 20,000 were reprinted, and in the end sales of the edition exceeded 100,000. This also included a three guinea limited edition of 1,240 on special hand-made paper. When Galsworthy came to the office to sign the copies of this special edition, he first asked how much he stood to gain on each book. The royalty being 20%, the answer was 12/6. After making a simple calculation, he took his watch out of his pocket, propped it on the desk and said, 'Let us see how long it will take me to earn £780.' A.G. Lewis, then the firm's manager, stood with the blotting paper poised to press on each copy; and with his help Galsworthy completed the task, without stopping, in two hours and ten minutes, eventually earning in today's money not less than £25,000.

Not surprisingly, author and publisher remained lifelong personal friends, and Anthony Powell, who was to play a part

John Galsworthy by Edward Burra, 1932.

in the firm's development in the late 1920s, has convincingly detected a similarity between Soames Forsyte and Gerald himself. He has also pointed out that Galsworthy's novels show 'a lack of any real understanding of human behaviour', and that 'his stylisation of character, and near-Marxist moralisings about the ownership of property, have the effect of heightening the drama at the expense of reality, and work better on the stage as a result'. It has also been noted that while Shaw made his characters speak in the way in which he himself thought, Galsworthy had the knack of making them talk like real people. *Strife, Loyalties* and *The Skin Game* continued to be sold all over the English-speaking world in large editions for use in schools, and made an important contribution to Duckworth's meagre profits. Further evidence of Gerald Duckworth's extensive and varied contacts at the time is provided by the fact that his very first list contained a slight story by Henry James called *In the Cage*, concerning the preoccupation of a girl working in a post office with a love affair being conducted, as was possible at the time, by telegram.

The connection with James seems to have petered out immediately, and of far greater importance for Duckworth was the appearance on their list of the first book by Elinor Glyn, a glamorous and extremely successful author who came to occupy a position somewhere between those of Nancy Mitford and Antonia Fraser half a century later. She was such a remarkable character, and was so profitable to Duckworth, that it is worth spending some time on her. After a strange upbringing, well described in her biography by her grandson Anthony Glyn, she had turned down a proposal of marriage from the Duke of Newcastle, because as she wrote later, 'he was absorbingly interested in the details of ecclesiastical apparel, and this subject was so far removed from my own ideas as to the things that matter most in life that I wonder that I appealed to him sufficiently to pay me such a compliment'. Instead, she married Clayton Glyn, a rich Essex landowner, generous, warm-hearted, conventional, but with a good sense of humour, which was extended to cover the antics of his wife's many admirers, and with a vast appetite for travel. To what extent he satisfied her passionate, idealistic nature is unclear, but in her fascinating, forthright memoirs she makes no criticism of his hopeless lack of any business sense whatsoever, which led to large personal debts and to eventual virtual bankruptcy. She seems to have accepted his shortcomings as other people accept the weather, writing of him with considerable affection, having cheerfully turned herself from a life of comparative idleness to becoming the breadwinner for the rest of his short life.

After the birth of her second daughter, Elinor had become seriously ill, and later developed rheumatic fever. It was while convalescing from this that she had the idea of rewriting parts of her diaries in the form of letters describing the goings-on in the exalted social circles in which she was very much at home, initially through a close friendship with Lady Warwick, whom she regarded as 'the most fascinating woman I have ever met'. The result was *The Visits of Elizabeth*, in which the central character is based loosely on Lady Angela St. Clair-Erskine, later for many years mistress of the Earl of Wemyss. She was also the sister of the Duchess of Sutherland and of Lady Westmorland, and a key member of Lady Warwick's circle. Lady Warwick herself, incidentally, despite being the chatelaine of Warwick Castle and one of the mistresses of King Edward VII, developed a strong social conscience and later stood, though she came at the bottom of the poll, as the local Labour candidate against Anthony Eden.

Elinor Glyn described in her memoirs an excellent example of the social and in this case clerical hypocrisy which she so detested and which was a common feature of the age.

> I remember one morning when Lady Warwick and I happened to be sitting in the saloon before anyone else was down, a new curate of one of her villages [*sic*] was shown in. He was a prim person, who fasted seriously in Lent. During conversation about the parish he mentioned that some ungodly people, non-churchgoers, were in trouble, and that the husband was very ill. It was God's judgement, he said, and they did not deserve help. Daisy listened with a far-away look that I knew well, and while carrying on the conversation with the curate about a new church hall which she was building, she leant over and rang the bell. When the footman appeared she told him to send the housekeeper, and she still went on talking sweetly to the curate. When the housekeeper arrived she looked up casually and telling her the names and address of the 'ungodly' wretches, she said 'I hear they are in great trouble. Please have beef tea and jellies and port sent round to them at once, and say that I will drive over and see them this afternoon.' Then she went on talking to the dumbfounded curate about the erection of the hall, as if nothing had happened.

Clayton Glyn, to help his wife with her long and otherwise helpless convalescence, showed the imaginary letters to an

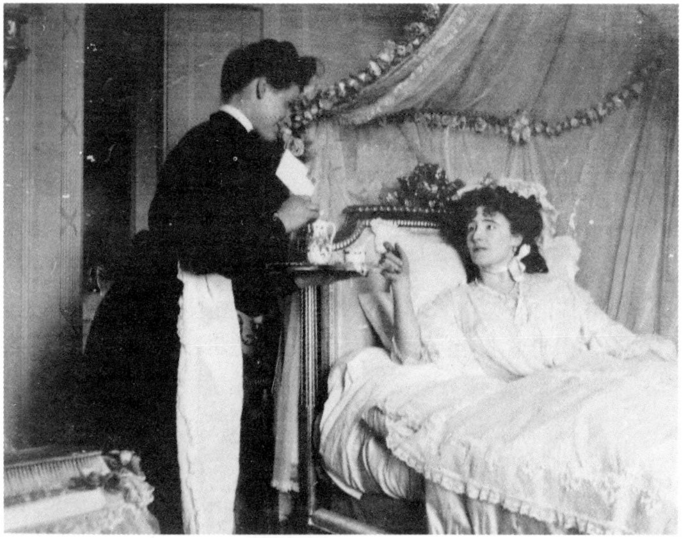

Top: Elinor Glyn, in a bed designed by her sister Lucy Duff Gordon.

Above: Sir Leslie Stephen by Sir William Rothenstein, c. 1903.

acquaintance of his in the Garrick Club who was deputy editor of *The Standard.* He in turn mentioned them to Gerald, who had only set up in business sixteen months before. A leading critic in the shape of W.H. Mallock was one of the first to praise the letters when they appeared in book form, and Elinor Glyn was well and truly launched, owing much of her initial success to a mischievous sense of fun combined with shrewd satire and a gentle warmth of heart. The book was serialised in *The World,* had an instant success and was reprinted several times by Milsted while Gerald himself was away in America. It has been well described as 'a hothouse romance of the highest, most luxurious and self-indulgent society'. But it was more than that. The author went on, in her memoirs, to describe the morals of high society (at a time when such a thing existed in a sense in which it largely ceased to do after 1918) and the sheer hypocrisy which characterised it. Adultery was common, but marriage with the rarest exceptions was a permanent institution, and divorce was not only very rare but certain to involve a considerable degree of social disgrace. Quite simply, it spelt the end of a woman's social career, and husbands, however erring, were seldom got rid of since life without them was so much worse, and consolation elsewhere in the meantime far from impossible. Always provided that conventional duties were observed, 'the emotional (and sexual) life of an individual was regarded as his or her own concern'. However imperfect the system, Elinor Glyn's feelings, many years later, were as follows:

> I have never been able to see how a ridiculous formality such as a few weeks' residence in Reno, coupled with the services of a good lawyer, can make any difference

> whatsoever to the morality or otherwise of becoming the mistress – or so-called wife – of another man, during the lifetime of your first husband. Such breaking of vows, I still believe, draws an inevitable nemesis, which cannot be exorcised by a mere legal formality, while the fundamental immorality of injuring husband and children by public divorce in order to be able to claim the joys of remarriage represents, I believe, a mere shirking of the issue, and it usually involves selfish behaviour and injury to others which is, I consider, far more immoral than the physical infidelity. I think it less wrong to remain content with an uneasy illicit relationship, and to renounce the joys of officially recognised marital relations for the sake of public decency, and the welfare of your children, than to clamour for a legal blessing which alters none of the facts and which is in reality nothing but a cowardly and childish effort to pass the responsibility for individual moral behaviour on to the shoulders of the Judiciary.

Such was the background against which her first two best-sellers were written, the second being *The Reflections of Ambrosine*, which contains a portrait of Daisy Warwick in Lady Tilchester. But in 1903, while searching for a new theme, she began to brood on the recent assassination of Queen Draga of Serbia, and in 1906, on a visit to Kintore Castle in Scotland, she was asked to brighten a wet evening by telling the assembled house party a story. She recalled the scene as follows:

> A handsome young man in a velvet smoking-suit was sprawling on a rug before the fire playing with a rough-haired terrier. He was the usual type of the young Englishman of the upper classes in those days, and unknown in any other country or period; a typical product of Eton and Oxford, endowed with a splendid physique, personal charm and innate good qualities of the highest order, but intellectually and emotionally sound asleep.
>
> I found myself wondering what such a young man might become if a really attractive woman who knew the world crossed his path. Suddenly it flashed into my mind that here was the ideal hero for the novel based on the murder of Queen Draga which I had been weaving, and I told the story of *Three Weeks* as we sat there round the fire. My imagination was fired, and I returned to Essex full of a desire to write the story as a book ... In six weeks the book was finished ... When it was finished I used to sit and stare into the fire for hours in a kind of trance. There was no detail that I could not visualise; no emotion I did not feel.

The novel pours out, in a raging torrent, the passionate imaginary affair, set in Switzerland, Venice and finally the coast of Dalmatia, between the young man on the Scottish hearthrug and Queen Draga. Given the name of Paul, he is reduced to a numb wreck when it is over and the Queen is dead, 'but his spirit was stamped with her nameless distinction', since while she was alive he swore to make no attempt to discover her identity. 'It was as if his judgement of life had now given him the key.' After the birth of his son to the hitherto childless Queen, she is murdered by the henchmen of her bestial husband, who bites the dust in his turn. Paul, after a period of broken-down dejection, is purged by loss and suffering, and wins through to a state of great moral regeneration, inspired by the heroic grandeur of his beloved; while his son, however improbably, is destined to reign with strength and wisdom over a pacified host of Balkan subjects. The book was widely condemned, especially by those who had not read it, or had not reached the end, as a celebration of illicit passion. But, for one thing, it dealt with what the author rather simply described afterwards as 'an unusual, Slavonic type of woman, and it did not pretend to lay down a model for the behaviour of an English schoolgirl'. Not long after its publication, and to her intense pleasure

> An old Scottish Professor of the History of Religions came to stay with us. [She was particularly addicted to the company of elderly academics.] He had heard the philistine view that it was a very bad book, and was prepared to chide me. I gave him a copy of the book, which like most of my critics he had never seen. He sat there in my sitting-room and read and read, forgetting even to come down for lunch, and when I went up to find him he was sitting head in hands, crying like a child. 'Lassie,' he said, 'I am ashamed of my thoughts on it yesterday. Posterity will justify you.'

The photograph reproduced on page 20 shows her lying in a bed designed by her sister Lucy, another remarkable character, who along with her husband Sir Cosmo Duff Gordon survived the *Titanic*. Being impecunious like her sister, she opened a dress shop called Lucile which later had branches in Paris, New York and Chicago, and played her part in the history of fashion by championing the divided skirt.

Such was Elinor Glyn, and such was *Three Weeks*. It was reprinted many times, and after a dormant period was reissued in 1974, with an introduction by Cecil Beaton, and a garish black and purple jacket which must have shaken that fastidious artist to the core. This is not the place to trace the rest of her life in detail; but she survived until 1943, having, after her husband's death, had a long affair with Lord Curzon, who treated her abominably, allowing her to become aware of his impending second marriage – he was a widower himself at the time of their liaison – by reading of it in *The Times*. She published many more novels, and had a successful career in Hollywood until the end of the silent film era. When introduced to Charlie Chaplin, she is alleged to have said, 'But you don't look nearly as funny as I expected!', and he to have replied, 'Neither do you.' One of her daughters, who married Sir Rhys Rhys Williams, became a Governor of the BBC and was made DBE as well as DStJ. If these achievements were less stirring than those of her mother's fictional heroines, she certainly inherited the dash and dedication that had gone into her mother's sparkling career. Far from being the sybarite or voluptuary which some of her novels might suggest, Elinor Glyn was a warm-hearted, adventurous idealist for whom no real parallel is to be found in women novelists since. It is worth noting that her grandson and biographer Anthony Glyn made a considerable name for himself as a writer: *The Dragon Variation* was praised in 1968 as one of the best literary dramas ever composed on the subject of chess, and as well as several other successful novels his exuberant *Companion Guide to Paris*, where he lived for some years, was well up to the standard of that invaluable series.

The firm of Duckworth was now well in business. But what

was its founder really like? If anyone has heard of him at all it is probably in relation to an incident which took place when he was sixteen and his half-sister Virginia was six. As she related many years later in 'A Sketch of the Past', he upset her terribly by standing her on a ledge and examining her private parts. A girl of more robust temperament might have shrugged this off; but not Virginia. Sensitive to the core, as well as highly perceptive and amusing, she seems never to have entirely recovered from the experience.

However, apart from this one childhood incident, Gerald was clearly kind and considerate. He gave Virginia a pound for her fifteenth birthday, and was full of concern for her in a slightly ridiculous and no doubt irritating way. In 1902 she recorded in another letter that 'Gerald has taken up with an American millionaire and is cruising with him down the coast of Italy. He meant to go to Venice, but the yacht was too tempting. "Everything is done in first-rate style." ' The next year, in May, 'Georgie and Gerald are out every night – balls and operas.' By then her father was not expected to live much longer, and in September she wrote, 'One thing is good. Gerald talked to Nessa [her sister Vanessa] and takes our view most strongly, says we must *of course* leave this house [in Hyde Park Gate] and he wants to take rooms separate. I believe he has wanted this a long time.' In 1904 the two sisters did in fact go to Venice with him, and Virginia wrote that 'there never was such an amusing and beautiful place. Gerald is bored to death, and very cross, and makes us take gondolas and doesn't like exploring back streets at all ... I think he will be glad to get safe to Monte Carlo.'

Later that year, on September 19, after spending a Sunday with Virginia, Gerald wrote to one of her dearest friends, Violet Dickinson, that Virginia's precarious nervous and mental state was improving.

> She is really a different creature and personally I think much more wholesome in mind than she has ever been – may it continue. I wrote to her today telling her to be like an elephant who always feels his way if there's the slightest doubt but she talked to me so clearly yesterday as to her feelings and what she thought and had experienced that it made me feel all was clear going now provided she does not overtax herself and that is the one thing to watch. Things are now on a satisfactory basis. What we owe you my dear Violet passes ink but we thank you and many good marks must have been registered by Paul or was it Peter.

Gerald's elephantine advice to Virginia, and his confusion between the Recording Angel and St. Peter at the pearly gates add a vivid flavour to his otherwise rather elusive personality. But it is interesting to note that many years later Virginia herself wrote to Violet Dickinson about this troubled time, saying, 'How very trying I was – all agog, aquiver, and so full of storms and "rhapsodies".' In December 1906 she wrote that 'Gerald has gone off to Egypt for a month. He wants to feel warm, and the Club fire won't do. Really, I love Gerald; he has been very sympathetic and useful all this time' (following her father's death). This last comment is an important antidote to the accepted view of Gerald, such as it is, as a stuffy and unimaginative plodder. It is also essential to remember that Virginia's sparkling letters were above all intended to entertain (at least when she was in

The wedding of Gerald Duckworth and Cecil Scott-Chad.

good spirits) with wild exaggerations and private jokes and references that the recipient would savour. They are not to be taken in deadly earnest, as serious historical evidence.

But as time went on, Gerald's limitations seem to have intensified, and whatever sense of curiosity and adventure he might once have had dwindled sadly. Undoubtedly there was a conventional and pompous, sometimes absurd (and increasingly idle) side to Gerald. But as the above shows, he was plainly kind-hearted, and prepared to take trouble with and for other people. At the age of fifty he made what proved to be a childless marriage, to Cecil Scott-Chad, who shared his still keen interest in the theatre. Her brother was the heir to the Pynkney estate in Norfolk, but as he had no children either, it was eventually inherited by a great-nephew of Gerald's, Anthony Duckworth, on condition that he added Chad to his surname. Gerald seldom visited Pynkney, having no interest in country pursuits, but was instrumental in bringing a handsome property into the family. Soames Forsyte would surely have approved. At any rate, in the year before Gerald's death in 1937, Virginia wrote to Violet Dickinson, 'Gerald I saw, for the first time these twenty years, the other day. I think he did well in his wife, but her task in keeping that lethargic alligator in being must be heroic. He had been ill. I rather think, as you say, he has the same affection for the bottle that George [who had died two years earlier] had for roast duck and spinach. But this is uncharitable.' Once again, this was written for the entertainment of a close friend, and to keep the sparks of intimacy flying. Anthony Powell, who appears later in this story, echoes this thought when he records that Gerald 'was reputed on a good day to put away a bottle of claret at lunch' at the Garrick. Back in 1907 Gerald had visited Virginia at Playden, and she wrote afterwards to Violet Dickinson: 'My spirits spring like fire now that he is gone!' Conversation had been sticky, until 'at last he fell asleep, as a prize pig, well entertained, might sleep. This is brutal, because he took a great deal of trouble to come; and I should be affectionate.' But, anyway at the time, she wasn't.

Altogether, the picture that emerges is of a solid, leisurely, prosperous, rather self-indulgent man, but honest and capable of shrewdness, susceptible to being entertained by novels and plays, and by their authors, conscious of social levels, and disapproving, in a way which may seem odd today but which was quite normal at the time, of social distinctions being ignored or violated. Stuffy but upright, and kind when he considered kindness due, but according to Powell, inclined to be obstructive and a bit of a *faux bonhomme*. Such was the founder of the firm. How amazed – and shocked – he would have been by the vicissitudes that it went through in the last quarter of its first century.

To return to the early lists, a good example of their catholicity is provided by the fact that cheek by jowl with Elinor Glyn stood the belligerent, stimulating figure of Hilaire Belloc. His *Cautionary Tales for Children*, though not published in one volume till 1912, began as doodles in the House of Commons, into which he was swept in the Liberal landslide of 1906. After four years, Belloc could no longer stand the hypocrisy of Parliament, and what he regarded as its refusal to address the important issues of the day. He memorably summed up the party system of the day in four lines 'On a General Election', almost certainly the one in which he himself was returned.

The accursed power which stands on Privilege
(And goes with Women and Champagne and Bridge)
BROKE – and Democracy resumed her Reign:
(Which goes with Bridge, and Women and Champagne.)

Another piece of advanced social comment ran as follows:

Lord Finchley tried to mend the electric light
Himself. It struck him dead, and serve him right.
It is the business of the wealthy man
To give employment to the Artisan.

The following is in a class of its own:

The Devil, having nothing else to do,
Went out to tempt my Lady Poltagrue;
My Lady, tempted by a private whim,
To his extreme annoyance tempted him.

Belloc's *Tales* remain superior to his earlier classic, *The Bad Child's Book of Beasts*, charming though that is in a simpler, less ambitious fashion. They still appeal enormously to children, and to those who are no longer children. Exquisitely constructed, with an uncanny feeling of words, they are also deft and telling, and easily memorised even by the scatter-brained. Who, once they have heard it, can forget that after naughty Matilda has set fire to her home,

At last the house began to fall!
It tottered, shuddering to and fro,
And fell into the street below,
Which happened to be Savile Row.

And even the greatest political ignoramus can hardly fail to be moved by the rebuke of the tearful Lord Lundy's grandsire:

Sir! You have disappointed us!
We had intended you to be
The next Prime Minister but three.
The stocks were sold; the Press was squared;
The Middle Class was quite prepared.
But as it is – my language fails!
Go out and govern New South Wales!

Earlier, at the time of the Boer War, *The Modern Traveller*, originally published by Arnold, but reissued by Duckworth many times, was an account in verse of the South African adventures of those bold buccaneers Commander Sin and Captain Blood. It contains the chilling couplet

Whatever happens, we have got
The Maxim Gun, and they have not.

One could go on quoting, but the reader is advised to acquire the books. Sadly, many years later the rights reverted to the author's estate, and the titles were eventually reissued by Jonathan Cape, and also by the Everyman Library, from whom they are now obtainable. The illustrations, by Belloc's friend Lord Basil Blackwood, are original, inventive and extremely amusing. But those who take the trouble usually have an even higher regard for Belloc's serious poems, which he published with Duckworth under the title *Verses* in 1910, and in expanded form, as *Sonnets and Verse*, in 1923. One of the former, on an untimely death, reveals his strengths and also his weaknesses.

Your life is like a little winter's day
Whose sad sun rises late to set too soon;
You have just come – why will you go away
Making an evening of what should be noon?
Your life is like a little flute complaining
A long way off, beyond the willow trees:
A long way off, and nothing left remaining
But memory of a music on the breeze.
Your life is like a pitiful leave-taking,
Wept in a dream before a man's awaking,
A call with only shadows to attend:
A Benediction whispered and belated
Which has no fruit beyond a consecrated,
A consecrated silence at the end.

The other chief strand in Belloc's poetry was inspired by a passionate love and loyalty for a particular stretch of country, based always on a penetrating study of its history, and a real gift for conjuring up its essence. His illuminating, and very charming, study of the French poets of the Renaissance, *Avril*, shows a perfect familiarity with Anjou, the Loire and Burgundy, and he later formed an equally intense devotion to the Pyrenees. But in England his attention was focused on Sussex, where in 1901 he and his wife for some reason bought a house, or rather a former village shop, at Shipley, near Horsham. It was curiously unsuited for human habitation, but he was in those days, and also later, never in one place for long enough for this to matter very much, at any rate to him. He was constantly striding over the Sussex Weald, either alone or in company with like-minded fellow-trampers, who had to share not only his great physical energy but his fondness for stopping at any congenial inn (and it was not often that one was not sufficiently congenial) for a considerable intake of Sussex beer, which for a time he insisted was superior to any other; though later in life he would cheerfully admit, 'It's all alcohol to me.' He wrote some delightful poems about Sussex, but there as elsewhere he often came close to self-parody. The mainspring of his life was his strong, unselfconscious religious faith, exemplified in the following ballade, which refers to the banning of a statue of the Madonna and Child by an Anglican bishop.

Ballade of Illegal Ornaments

The controversy was ended by His Lordship, who wrote to the Incumbent ordering him to remove from the church all illegal ornaments at once, and especially a Female Figure with a Child.

When that the Eternal deigned to look
On us poor folk to make us free,
He chose a Maiden, whom he took
From Nazareth to Galilee
Since when the Islands of the Sea
The Field, the City and the Wild
Proclaim aloud triumphantly
A Female Figure with a Child.

These mysteries profoundly shook
The Reverend Doctor Leigh, D.D.,
Who therefore stuck into a nook
(or Niche) of his Incumbency
An Image filled with Majesty
To represent the Undefiled,
The Universal Mother – She –
A Female Figure with a Child.

Hilaire Belloc on the Nona.

His Bishop, having read a book
Which proved as plain as plain could be
That all the Mutts had been mistook
Who talked about a Trinity,
Wrote off at once to Doctor Leigh
In manner very far from mild,
And said 'Remove them instantly!
A Female Figure with a Child!'

Envoi
Prince Jesus, in mine Agony,
Permit me, broken and defiled,
Through blurred and glazing eyes to see
A Female Figure with a Child.

Belloc's later political and historical ramblings were often inaccurate in the extreme, repetitive, and ultimately tedious. But just as, a generation later, De Gaulle had *une certaine idée de la France,* so Belloc had a certain idea of Europe, and of its redemption by the Catholic Faith after the onslaughts of the pagan Goths and Vandals and Norsemen. But his deep devotion to the Faith did not prevent him from attacking its guardians, and generations of Catholics, especially in recent years, have derived great comfort and reassurance from his observation that 'the Catholic Church is divine, and the proof of it I take to be this, that no purely human organisation, conducted with such knavish imbecility, would have lasted more than five minutes'. His genius lay in 'feeling his way into the past', as his biographer A.N. Wilson has aptly put it, and in drawing his readers in with him. But he was not always inclined to make himself agreeable, especially after disappointments and sorrows of various kinds had piled up. Anthony Powell later described him coming into the office to collect copies of his books, wearing an Inverness Cape and (leather) Wellington boots under his trousers, grumpy, bad mannered. It seems likely, too, that he suffered, or fancied he suffered, in some way from having a French name, when after the early death of his father, his English mother brought him up resolutely in England, where his restless future was to remain based. Perhaps for this reason, he insisted on his name appearing on all his books as H. Belloc, to avoid using his French Christian name; and he was known to his friends by its anglicised form of Hilary.

Religious enthusiasm of a very different kind from Belloc's inspired a series which Duckworth brought out under the title Studies in Theology. The editor was Dr. Stuart J. Reid, and the books consisted of biblical studies intended chiefly for an interdenominational readership. He was succeeded as editor by Dr. A.W. Harrison, Principal of Westminster College, and later by Dr. Nathaniel Micklem, Principal of Mansfield College. The names of most of the authors would mean nothing to today's readers, with the possible exception of Dr. Hastings Rashdall, and W.R. Inge, the rather unfairly nicknamed 'Gloomy Dean' of St. Paul's. But the books were regularly reprinted, and provided steady business for the firm. There was also a series of popular lives of the saints, relying heavily on French priests as authors, but also including the Duc de Broglie on St. Ambrose. By 1912, the series comprised twenty-two volumes. A later series, the Colet Library of Modern Christian Thought and Teaching, took shape after 1939, for use by laymen, with an emphasis on the provision of guidance on the relevance of Christianity to contemporary needs and problems.

Earlier still, a series called the Popular Library of Art was edited by Mrs. Strong, wife of the Librarian of the House of Lords. In the days when the history of art was very much a minority interest, these monographs were of considerable value. They included works on *Donatello, Six Greek Sculptors, Michelangelo,* and *The School of Ferrara.* But for some reason the series was dropped in 1911. Another independent spirit, restless as Belloc and never happier than when roaming the countryside, was W.H. Davies, who published three books with Duckworth. As far as his verse goes, he is perhaps best remembered for a naïve poem with the rather flat title 'Leisure', deeply unfashionable now, but effective and appealing in its day, and much anthologised.

> What is this life, if, full of care,
> We have no time to stand and stare?
> No time to stand beneath the boughs
> And stare as long as sheep or cows.
> No time to see, when woods we pass,
> Where squirrels hide their nuts in grass.
> No time to see, in broad daylight,
> Streams full of stars, like skies at night.
> No time to turn at Beauty's glance,
> And watch her feet, how they can dance.
> No time to wait till her mouth can
> Enrich that smile her eyes began.
> A poor life this, if full of care
> We have no time to stand and stare.

His prose *Autobiography of a Super-Tramp* was also offered to Duckworth. But Bernard Shaw, a keen admirer of Davies, who wrote an introduction to the book, very characteristically interfered with the details offered in the contract. Shaw, ever watchful on behalf of authors, always chose to ignore the financial risk taken by publishers, and regarded them as nothing more than author's agents. Among other things he insisted, on behalf of Davies, that Duckworth should only have a licence to publish the book for three years, and also claimed for the author the right to approve or reject illustrations, cover design and even advertising lay-outs, and also to be released from the normal libel clause.

Not unnaturally, Duckworth refused all these changes from normal practice. The book was published by Fifield, and in 1917 by Knopf in America, where it eventually sold over 10,000 copies. Nevertheless, Davies was perpetually, and not surprisingly, hard up. Some of his friends, impressed by the *Autobiography*, arranged for him to be offered a small sinecure at the British Museum, with a modest income in exchange for the lightest of duties. Davies was not pleased. He complained later to Richard Church, 'They expected me to work! I have never worked in my life. That's what your friends do for you!' Nevertheless he was granted a Civil List pension by the Prime Minister, Asquith, and a grant from the Royal Literary Fund.

At the time, there was plainly a big demand for good descriptions of the countryside, and of travels in remote places. As early as 1902, Duckworth took on W.H. Hudson's *El Ombu*, a book of short stories which Heinemann had turned down but which remained the author's own favourite among his South American romances. Two years later, they reissued another of his successes, *The Purple Land,* together with a new book which became one of his best known, *Green Mansions,* and Hudson, not altogether an easy character, later recalled the pleasure he had been given by his regular lunches with Garnett at the Mont Blanc in Gerrard Street. This restaurant was for some years the venue for a more or less regular lunch for Duckworth authors every Tuesday. It seems unlikely that Gerald himself attended these occasions, feeling as he did more at home at his clubs. The Garrick was only two hundred yards from the office, and he also belonged to the Savile and the Bath, and at one time or another served on the committees of all three. Presumably Garnett was the leading spirit on the home team at these lunches, and certainly it was he who had the most to offer in the way of a helping hand for authors who might temporarily have ground to a halt.

As well as Hudson's books, and roughly in the same genre, Duckworth also reissued, in the cheap editions which had now come to the fore, three books by Richard Jefferies which had first appeared under a different imprint: *Amaryllis at the Fair, After London or Wild England,* and the evergreen classic *Bevis, the Story of a Boy.* Hudson's wonderful *A Shepherd's Life*, an evocative description of the South Wiltshire Downs, was for some reason allowed to appear on another list, as was *Birds and Man,* an eloquent book, well ahead of its time in protesting against the robbing of rare bird's nests for the benefit of egg-collectors, and the killing, sometimes to the point of extinction, of other rarities for display in glass cases or on women's hats. The Greens of today might well look back on him as one of their earliest post-industrial champions.

Another distinct strand in the Duckworth tapestry before 1914 was the Russian one. It began with the publication in 1903 of the first volume of Chekhov's short stories to appear in English, itself probably following on from the plays by Ibsen and Strindberg which Gerald had taken on earlier. There was also a book of stories by Maxim Gorky, including the grim but emotionally penetrating *Twenty-six Men and a Girl* (1902), which gave its name to the volume. This in turn led to the anarchist Kropotkin's *Ideals and Realities in Russian Literature,* and in due course to further stories and plays by Chekhov, including *The Seagull* and *Uncle Vanya* in 1912. As a contribution to the Edwardian cultural scene, all this was certainly something to be proud of, especially from a standing start only a few years previously.

But it was not only a matter of slim volumes of poetry and plays and travellers' tales. In 1906 Duckworth took what must have been a considerable risk in bringing out, in six volumes, an epic poem by Charles Doughty called *The Dawn in Britain.* This was certainly one of Garnett's bolder strokes. He described it fearlessly as 'the greatest poem since *Paradise Lost*', though it was in fact through Milsted that the manuscript, in the author's tiny handwriting, reached the firm. The style now seems impenetrably archaic and obscure, and it was the publication in 1908 of *Wanderings in Arabia* that first brought the author popular success. This was a two-volume abridgement of his massive *Travels in Arabia Deserta,* first brought out in an edition of 500 copies by the Cambridge University Press in 1888, and dormant ever since. This was followed by further poems, *Adam Cast Forth* (1908), *The Cliffs* (1909), *The Clouds* (1912), and *The Titans* (1916). In more down to earth vein, Duckworth also published O. Kellner's *The Scientific Feeding of Animals,* and *The Golf Courses of the British Isles,* by Bernard Darwin and Harry Rountree. Distancing himself from the output of other members of his family, Darwin was to become the doyen of British writers on golf, and was still hard at it fifty years later. By contrast, Edward Thomas and Walter de la Mare also published their first volumes of poetry with the firm, *Rose Acre Papers* and *The Three Mulla-Mulgars* respectively. As all this shows, no real pattern had emerged on the Duckworth list before the war: just about anything that took the fancy of Garnett or the Directors seems to have been acceptable, but in nearly every case the quality remained either genuinely high, or at least in accordance with enlightened popular taste.

But perhaps the best known author that Garnett befriended and brought in for a time was D.H. Lawrence, who addressed him simply as 'My dear Authority'. His novel *The Trespasser* was published in 1912, and he wrote to Garnett on September 16 from Lake Garda that 'this morning Duckworth sent me £50 in notes – the angel! We are both bursting with joy and puffed up in importance. Also we've got a place to live in.' In the following year, 1913, Duckworth published Lawrence's *Love Poems* and also *Sons and Lovers*, and in 1914 *The Widowing of Mrs. Holroyd* and *The Prussian Officer and Other Stories.* In April 1914 Lawrence wrote again to Garnett:

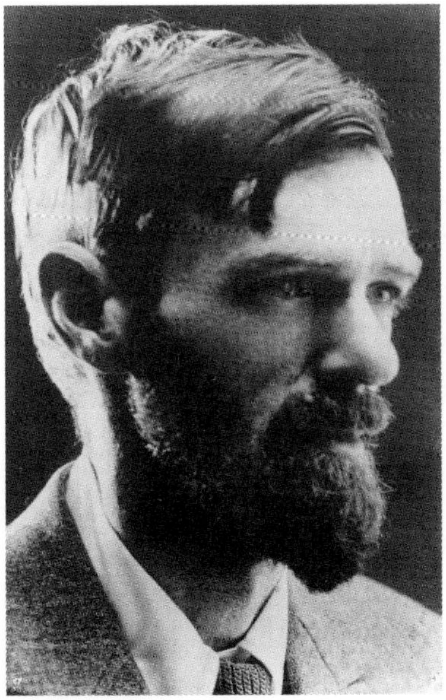

D.H. Lawrence.

> it was horrid to receive the accounts for *Sons and Lovers* [published the year before] and to see that Duckworth had lost a number of pounds on the book – fifteen or so, was it? That is very unpleasant. ... If a publisher is to lose by me, I would rather it were a rich commercial man like Heinemann ...
>
> If Duckworth is not really *keen* on this next novel [*The Rainbow*] we will give it to Pinker [a literary agent]. I don't think I want to sign an agreement for another novel after this. I did not like to see that he [i.e. Duckworth] had lost on *Sons and Lovers.* And I *must* have money to live. And if the other publishers definitely offer, they who are commercial people, whereas you are my friend – well, they may lose as much as they like.

Such sentiments are, to put it mildly, unlikely to be heard today, and show Lawrence in a distinctly attractive light, as do many of his other personal letters. His trouble was an obsession with getting his own way, and an utter refusal to compromise, either over important issues or trifles. Like other authors, he was much concerned with the promotion of his books, and wrote to Garnett in 1913: 'If *Hamlet* and *Oedipus* were published now they wouldn't sell more than 100 copies unless they were pushed.' As Colin Haycraft, a later Chairman of Duckworth, observed, 'Hype springs eternal.' When crossed, Lawrence could become a howling banshee, as the following indicates, in an earlier letter to Garnett:

> Why, why and why was I born an Englishman! My cursed, rotten-boned, pappy hearted countrymen, why was I sent to them?
>
> Curse the blasted, jelly-boned swines, the slimy, belly-wriggling invertebrates, the miserable sodding rotters, the flaming sods, the snivelling, dribbling, dithering, palsied, pulseless lot that make up England today. They've got white of egg in their veins, and their spunk is that watery it's a marvel they can breed .... God blast them, wish-wash. Exterminate them, slime.

Nevertheless, even after *The Rainbow* had gone to Methuen, it was Duckworth who in 1916 published Lawrence's *Amores* and also *Twilight in Italy*.

It would be impossible to imagine a greater contrast between the explosive, sometimes virulent vitality of Lawrence, the Nottingham miner's son, and another author who first appeared on the Duckworth list in 1913, the year between the two Lawrence novels just mentioned. Maurice Baring was a junior, non-practising member of the banking family, a close friend of Belloc, and by now a fellow-Catholic. His *Lost Diaries* show his extraordinary powers of imagination, and especially his insight into the characters and possible feelings of historical figures, and his timeless wit and lightness of touch in representing them. Other passages are equally good, but one of those that have best stood the test of time is the following extract from the diary of William the Conqueror. Baring was an accomplished French scholar, a close friend of Sara Bernhardt, and as much at home in Paris as in London. Here, he transposes French attitudes to the English on the eve of the Great War to the time of the Norman Conquest.

> *Rouen,* 1066. Disquieting news from London. My friend, benefactor and relation, my brother Sovereign, Edward of England, has again had one of his attacks. Have the utmost confidence in Harold; but I fear the influence of the English nobility. I like the English; but they are not to be trusted in foreign politics. They are naturally perfidious, and they don't know it.
>
> Among other things, Father Anselm writes that a certain party among the English want to be admitted to the Witenagemot. The majority of the women are against it. The agitators sent a deputation to Westminster, but the King said it would not be according to the precedents to receive them. They were so annoyed at this that they made a dastardly attack on the beautiful old Druid Temple of Stonehenge, almost completely destroying it. F. Anselm says only a few blocks of stone are left, and that the place is unrecognisable.
>
> The ringleaders were taken and claimed the ordeal by fire and the matter was referred to the Archbishop of Canterbury, who said it was not a matter to be dealt with by ordeal. (Quite right!) He put the case into the hands of a select body of matrons, chosen from all classes. These decided that the offenders should be publicly whipped by women, and sent home. This was done, much to the satisfaction of everybody.
>
> *Rouen.* Heard Mass and went out hunting. Excellent sport. Shot a fox and six thrushes. Had thrush-pie for dinner. Find it difficult to get on horseback without aid.

Received a letter from the Pope. He says that should anything happen to King Edward – he is, of course, far from suggesting such a thing, but one has to take everything into consideration – I must be very firm claiming the succession. H.H. says that although, of course, it would be indelicate for him to raise the question *just now*, he knows it is the King's wish that I should succeed him. He seems to think Harold may give trouble. But Harold is bound to me by oath. Also I saved his life.

Rouen. The regular courier did not arrive this evening. The bag was brought by an Englishman. The official bulletin states that the King is slightly indisposed owing to a feverish cold, which he caught while inspecting the newly-raised body of archers, in the New Forest. A private letter from the Archbishop tells me, in strict confidence, that the King's illness is more dangerous than people think. The children again quarrelled today. Matilda, as usual, took Henry's part, and said I was to blame. These domestic worries are very trying at such a critical moment. As a matter of fact, Henry teases his elder brothers, and boasts to them of his superior scholarship; they retaliate, naturally enough, by cuffing the boy, who complains at once to his mother. Since Henry has mastered the rudiments of the alphabet, his conceit has been quite beyond bounds. Of course, I admit it is clever of him. There is no doubt about that, but he shouldn't take advantage of it.

Rouen. Again the regular courier has not arrived. The bag was again brought by an Englishman. According to a bulletin the King is going on well.

Rouen. Matilda says I must invade England at once. Think she is right. But wish war could be avoided. Have written to the Pope asking for his moral support. Invasion is a risky thing. Discussed the matter with General Bertram, who is an excellent strategist. He says he can devise fifty ways of landing troops in England, but not one way of getting them out again. That is just it. Supposing we are cut off? The English army is said to be very good indeed.

Rouen. Received letter from the Pope entirely approving of invasion. Received a letter from Harold also. Very insulting. Answers vaguely and commits himself to nothing. Ignores the past. Seems to forget I saved him from shipwreck, and that he solemnly swore to support my claims. Seems also to forget that I am the lawful heir to the English throne. The crowning insult is that he addressed the letter to Duke William the Bastard.

Have ordered mobilisation to take place. Matilda and I were loudly cheered when we drove through the market place this afternoon. War will be a good occupation for the boys. Robert wants to stop here as Regent. Do not think this wise.

London. Everything sadly in need of thorough reorganisation. Have resolved to carry out following initial reforms at once.

1. Everybody to put out their lights by 8. Bell to ring for the purpose. The people here sit up late, too late, drinking. Most dangerous.

2. Enroll everybody in a book. Make it compulsory for the leeches to attend the poor, and dock serfs of a part

'The Accompanist Who Did Her Best'
from Burlesques *by H.M. Bateman.*

of their wage, in order to create a fund for paying the leeches (Think this rather neat.)

When war came, in the following year, Milsted joined the Artillery, and Gerald, who was then forty-three, and beyond military age, was nevertheless conventionally determined to play his part, and succeed in working for two years at the Ministry of Munitions. He returned to the firm in 1916, when Cape, who had been in sole charge of day-to-day matters since the war began, was conscripted into the army. Virginia Woolf's first two novels, straightforward and arguably her best, were published by Gerald: *The Voyage Out* (1915) and *Night and Day* (1919). With her husband Leonard she started a small printing press, the Hogarth Press, chiefly as a therapy after the nervous breakdown she suffered between 1913 and 1915, after having for a time recovered from the mental troubles referred to earlier. By 1922 they were publishers as well as printers, and decided to bring out her novels under their own imprint. In Leonard's words, 'We went to see Gerald Duckworth who was extremely nice about it ... we bought back the rights in and stock of the two books he had published for later on when we wanted to publish them in uniform edition.' He also gave the sales figures for *Night and Day* during the ten years that it remained on Duckworth's list, and they are of some interest, especially in the absence of any other sales figures for the period: 1,767 copies were sold in the British Empire at 9/-, and 566 copies in a cheaper edition at 3/6d. The total American sales were 1,326, and the author's royalties over the whole period amounted to just under £150. It was quite a modest beginning.

Few traces of Duckworth's other publications during the war have survived, but in 1916 they brought out their only book by a brilliant comic artist – far more than a caricaturist, though he excelled in that as well – in the shape of *Burlesques* by H.M. Bateman. Later to become a national institution, he was in a variety of ways eccentric enough to be entirely appropriate for the Duckworth list. Sadly, his next eight books of cartoons were published by Methuen between 1921 and 1931, another example of a quite exceptional talent escaping from Duckworth and moving on elsewhere. Since he only produced a single book for them it would be wrong to devote too much space to him here, especially as no record survives of who took him on (probably Milsted) or why he left (possibly Gerald). His gifts of imagination were matched by a talent for line which probably owed something both to Aubrey Beardsley and to Phil May. He could take his subjects from the most mundane walks of real life and give them a drama and originality which was the fruit of true genius. His observations are not so much of individuals as of situations, which start by being ordinary and suddenly take off onto a meteoric course of fantasy and acquire a wild and uncontrollable momentum of their own, often in a series of fifteen or twenty scenes, ending either in an explosion or a collapse when the bubble bursts. He was in fact one of the forerunners of the animated cartoon film, and was much admired by Walt Disney, who on one of Bateman's American tours allowed him to watch the animators at work on their drawings in the Disney studios. As well as situations, Bateman dealt in types: when he created a plumber, as his agent A.E. Johnson remarked in an introduction to *Burlesques,* it was more like a plumber than any plumber ever was. Whatever the reason for his departure, it turned out to be one of Duckworth's greatest losses.

Roger

SOME BRIGHT SPARKS
1919-1931

Another great opportunity was lost in 1919, probably by the prudence of Gerald himself, but understandably in view of the shortage of working capital at his disposal, when T.E. Lawrence suggested that they should reissue the complete unabridged text of Doughty's *Arabia Deserta*. As has been mentioned, the firm had brought out a two-volume abridgement of this massive work in 1908, under the title *Wanderings in Arabia*. But for the entire work, typesetting alone would have cost the colossal sum for those days of £1,500, and it was hardly surprising that Gerald cautiously declined.

In 1920, denied a directorship by Gerald, Cape left to found his own firm at 30 Bedford Square, where it flourished exceedingly (with a slight downturn in the late 1950s) for over half a century. He very bravely launched his list with the full text of *Travels in Arabia Deserta* at the very high price of nine guineas, or about £300 in today's money. Lawrence's own personal mystique had arisen from his war record, blowing up Turkish troop trains and drumming up Arab support for the allies. It was also much enhanced by a flair for publicity for which he took care to seem reluctant. Together with Gertrude Bell, he had created a considerable vogue for Arabia and the Arabs, very different from the minority interest shown in them before the war. Cape founded the fortunes of his firm on this initial production and later reissued it in cheaper editions. About this time, too, Duckworth turned down James Joyce's *Portrait of the Artist as a Young Man* – as did no fewer than twenty-one other publishers.

Cape was succeeded as general manager by G. Belton Cobb, who in turn left after two years to join Longmans Green. Gerald was by this time looking for a new partner to inject fresh capital. He was lucky enough in 1923 to recruit Thomas Balston, a man who had been decorated with the O.B.E. and the M.C. in the war, and had learned publishing before 1914 with the firm of T. Fisher Unwin (known irreverently by him as the Fishy Onion) which had published, among other successes, the early works of Joseph Conrad. On becoming a partner he brought in another member of his old firm, A.G. Lewis. In 1925 the partnership between Gerald and Milsted was converted into a limited company. Gerald owned 7,000 shares, Balston 6,000 and Milsted 6,860. Dividends were paid, at 5% in 1926, 8% in 1927, 2% in 1929, and no less than 14% in the year 1930-31.

Both these newcomers, as well as Milsted, have happily been described in some detail in *Messengers of Day*, an autobiographical work by the novelist Anthony Powell, who was recruited to the firm three years later by Balston, a friend of his father's. Powell was then recently down from Oxford, and had a number of friends with literary

Edith Sitwell by Roger Fry.

aspirations, including Henry Yorke, who as Henry Green was to publish a number of novels highly regarded in certain circles. Powell later recollected that he 'could conjure up no more plausible means of attempting to earn a living'. He shared a room in the office with Lewis, and was sufficiently struck by his character to describe it in some detail, as will be seen in due course. Gerald had prudently acquired a ninety-nine-year lease, at a fixed rent of £500 a year, on 3 Henrietta Street, Covent Garden, and Powell describes the offices as by then, partly no doubt as a result of wartime restrictions that had never been subsequently adjusted, 'dingy within, only a few finely ornate door-fittings recalled better days'. He still remembers Gerald 'moving gloomily through the office, a haze of port-fumes and stale cigar-smoke in his wake', and that 'his interest in books, anyway as a medium for reading, was as slender as that of any man I have ever encountered'. Powell goes on to recapture vividly the distinctively un-vivid atmosphere of the office, or at least as it seemed to a member of a younger generation more than usually remote from the previous one. Gerald actually shared a room with Milsted, who by this time only occupied it on average one day a week, except when working on proofs, an activity over which he took much trouble and was well qualified. 'Their roll-top desks were set back to back ... hidden from each other by a towering wall of dust-covered books ... with more books and manuscripts, usually a newspaper or two, littering the floor round Gerald's seat, beside which, for the use of callers, stood an armchair in the last stages of decomposition. Dust was everywhere, disorder infinite.' But on the older inhabitants, the general shabbiness had probably crept up imperceptibly, and was now no doubt taken for granted.

Powell also gives a lively impression of Milsted, Gerald's second-in-command, who had joined the firm back in 1900, and was to remain in it for over fifty years. His manner is described as 'quiet and cordial', but his appearance, anyway at that time, suggested the racecourse, or the coaching club, more than the publisher's office: loud tweeds, year in, year out, and a brown bowler hat. His favourite dictum is said to have been, 'As long as a man owns a horse, a gun and a dog, he has no cause to complain of his lot.' All the same, he was well up to correcting Ronald Firbank's Latin, not only in his description of the last rites of the Church being administered to the Archduchess in *The Flower Beneath the Foot*, but also in the rather surprising exchanges between the footmen in *Valmouth*. Balston, on the other hand, was passionately dedicated to all the details of publishing , and had the sense of commitment needed for the task of building up what was, at least in the eyes of the youthful Powell, a thoroughly tumbledown concern. He described Balston as follows:

> Tall, thin, black moustached, jet black hair standing on end, Balston, then in his middle forties, gave expression to a mass of nervous tensions. He moved with jerky precipitancy, never closing a door without slamming it. Something of a classical scholar in his youth, other literary tastes were less easy to define. A delight in argument and contradiction required such preferences to be varied from hour to hour; sometimes total reversal of his normal point of view on any given subject. On the one hand, he favoured modernism, being attracted by any chance of shocking the old-fashioned or strait-laced with perverse philosophic, political, above all anti-religious views; on the other hand, too much sexual frankness could provoke in him embarrassed giggles.

Top left: Anthony Powell, at the time when he worked at Duckworth.

Top right: Tom Balston, later a director of Duckworth from 1923 to 1934.

Right: G.H. Milsted (holding the reins) on a coaching expedition.

If this description is at all accurate, Balston must often have been a maddening colleague, especially to someone of Gerald's proclivities. But, as will be seen in connection with Edith Sitwell, there was much more to Balston than the jumpy, self-contradicting figure just described. For one thing, one of his major interests was in wood engravings, and it was thanks to him that Duckworth became one of the first publishers to revive them as a medium of illustration. Several artists later to become very well known had their early work commissioned by the firm, including Paul Nash, Robert Gibbings, Eric Ravilious and Clare Leighton.

It is worth noting too that at the time when Powell worked at Duckworth, the firm published his own first four novels, *From a View to a Death*, *Agents and Patients*, *Afternoon Men* and *Venusberg*. A fifth, *What's Become of Waring?*, was published in 1939, in which much of the action concerns a publisher's office easily recognisable (from *Messengers of Day*) as Duckworth's. It is not fanciful to regard the two brothers who were partners in the fictional version, Bernard and Hugh Judkins, as being based on the figures of Gerald himself, in his later years, and Balston. There is, not surprisingly, no direct physical resemblance; or rather, Gerald's own characteristics appear to have been transposed onto Hugh, who is described as having 'a thin moss of sandy hair, where his head was not bald, and flashing rimless pince-nez which he wore lashed to one ear with a chain'. In the novel, Bernard/Gerald constantly refused to publish authors that Hugh/Balston wanted to take on, and 'spent most of the day dozing or conning the weekly papers'.

> Although Bernard put up a show of disagreeing with Hugh's decisions, on matters of importance he was unwilling to make any of his own. Sometimes he modified orders that Hugh had given. This was usually to cause petty annoyance rather than to indicate a change of policy .... It was unusual for him to express a wish to see anyone in the afternoon, which he was accustomed to spend in a state of comatose disapproval of modern life. Bernard's desk was at right angles to the window. Behind it he had made a nest for himself, a refuge against the world, where he could recapture some vestiges of prenatal irresponsibility. A broad parapet of books stretched across the top of the desk. Another similar but higher ran along the ledge of the window, so that he could neither see out of it nor be seen from the square. The shelves of another bookcase at his back tipped forward waywardly as if at any moment they might void their contents on his head. His fourth and most vulnerable side was protected by newspapers thrown about on the floor in such quantities that they formed a sort of a pyramid. Everything round him was covered with dust. A faint reminiscence of stale vegetables hung about the room, generated by old books and cigar-smoke.

This sounds like something in the nature of a parting shot from Powell, who by then had wearied of what was to him a thoroughly depressing and negative atmosphere, though to those who had spent much of their working lives there it no doubt represented something very different. Powell had left to take up a nebulous-sounding job in films, but it is not difficult to see why he preferred to publish his fifth novel elsewhere after Gerald Duckworth's death. Besides physical descriptions of the kind just quoted, the novel contains other observations relevant to Duckworth in the late 1920s, as when Hugh Judkins remarks to the narrator that 'making a literary reputation had never been so easy as in the first dozen years after the war, nor keeping one so difficult'. In fact, however, Powell's early days in the firm, though he never records them with enthusiasm or even animation – hardly, after all, his style – had been extremely productive, and had seen the recruitment of several of the best and brightest young authors of the decade, mostly his own contemporaries, and acquaintances, if not actually friends; though how much of the credit for this is his, and how much Balston's, is not clear. He probably introduced them, and whether or not they were taken on depended on the level of Balston's support in each individual case, and his ability to counteract Gerald's torpid disapproval of the rising stars who now began to join the list, namely the Sitwells, Harold Acton, Evelyn Waugh, Robert Byron and Roger Fulford.

Before going on to his own contemporaries, Powell also describes in his memoirs some of the better known Duckworth authors of the older generation whom he came across, usually very peripherally, at the time, including Galsworthy, who 'gave off the redolence of boundless vanity, a condition not uncommon among authors, in this case more noticeable than usual'. And Ford Madox Ford, whose 'immense self-pity', and 'misunderstandings and sentimentalities on the subject of English life' Powell criticises rather ungenerously, while admitting that 'he seemed amiable enough in a somewhat bufferish genre'. He also passes over the fact that Ford, who was forty-one, far above military age, had volunteered in 1914, joined the Welch Regiment, been shell-shocked in 1916 and invalided home. Another Duckworth author was Hugh Kingsmill, later rescued from oblivion by a biography by Michael Holroyd. Powell makes him seem a much more rewarding figure than, for instance, the repulsive-sounding black magician Aleister Crowley. Malcolm Muggeride also, in his published diaries, makes Kingsmill sound distinctly endearing.

But of all the new authors introduced by Balston and Powell, the Sitwells, between them, came to occupy the most prominent position in the literary world. That is not to say that they were the most profitable, either to themselves or to their publishers. Osbert, Edith and Sacheverell Sitwell had already been published by Grant Richards, a man of flair but with little business sense. When his firm became insolvent, there were naturally other publishers sniffing around to pick up the authors who had become homeless. In the case of the Sitwells, Balston outstripped his rivals by hurrying off to Amalfi, where the trio were engaged on a 'working' holiday, and signing them up on the spot.

In order to understand their attitudes and activities, it is necessary to look at their early lives. Their parents, Sir George and Lady Ida, had shown a good deal more than the general upper class indifference to their children's well-being that was so common at the time. They certainly received no encouragement to pursue their budding interests; and so they had naturally clung together from an early age, and developed an excessive mutual devotion and an exaggerated regard for each other's talents, especially in the case of Edith for Sachie, as he was always known. The crucial point was reached in 1914-15, when their parents were submerged in a hideous series of lawsuits against Lady Ida, the wife of the eccentric, selfish and unreasonable but by no means stupid Sir George. In despair at the debts which she had thoughtlessly amassed, and not daring to admit them to him, she had gone to unscrupulous money-lenders and had been prosecuted, and actually imprisoned, for fraud, at a time when Sachie was still at Eton, and Osbert, seven years older, was at the front in France with the Grenadiers, in constant and acute danger of his life. All this had greatly increased their insecurity and isolation, and added to their intense emotional interdependence. It was quite on the cards that the scandal would cause Sachie to be removed from Eton, where he was far from being a conventionally successful or happy schoolboy, and that Osbert would have to resign from his regiment, though in the end neither of these disasters occurred.

When the war was over, and after Sachie's very brief spell at Oxford, they all three threw themselves into the general mood which had sprung up in 'advanced' circles, of enthusiasm for aesthetic novelty in a variety of fields. This had of course existed before the war, for example in the Diaghilev ballets, and to some extent in the Post-Impressionist painters shown in Roger Fry's famous exhibition in 1913. During the war, however, the quest for colour and artistic adventure had been swamped by the casualty lists and the privations of wartime London. But when the war was at last over, the Sitwells had put themselves in the forefront of its revival. In spite of their tender years, they pursued it with energy, panache and generosity, and for a time carried all before them in the cultural field. Their enthusiasms included painting (Picasso, Modigliani, Severini and others), music (Satie, Stravinsky and especially Walton, who they housed in London), and above all Diaghilev's new ballet (Picasso again, Bakst, Derain). Most of the older generation regarded these new ideas and experiments as rubbish, and none more firmly than Gerald Duckworth. As usual with the avant garde, its champions were often looked on as affected poseurs and fools. These reactions, needless to say, had the effect of making the Sitwells close ranks with even greater determination than ever against the philistines, who in turn regarded them with increased disapproval. This was certainly the view of Gerald. Not that he was entirely philistine: it was simply that the post-war world was outside his comprehension, or perhaps his interest. What he much preferred was another afternoon of bridge at the Garrick, another glass of port, another good cigar, then back to the office to sign a few letters, then perhaps the first night of a conventional play. It was a habit-forming existence, harmless, but most unlikely to keep a publishing firm from growing stale and listless, along with its founder.

Later on, naturally, during and after the slump, in the proletarian mood of the thirties, the Sitwells were to reap the whirlwind which they had helped to sow. They came to be regarded not only as elitist (a word not yet used as a general term first of envy and later of unthinking abuse) but as irrelevant and largely meaningless. They seemed to be fiddling while millions of unemployed were hungry and desperate. Nor was there any question of their changing their tune and adapting to a different *Zeitgeist* from the one in which they had flourished earlier.

Back in 1923, Duckworth had taken over all the novels and short stories by Osbert Sitwell that had already been published by Grant Richards, including *Triple Fugue*, *Before the Bombardment*, and *The Man Who Lost Himself*. Later, there was a volume of travel and art commentary, *Winters of Content* (1932), which was reissued after the next war. And in 1943, when his prose works had been moved to Macmillan, Duckworth still published his *Selected Poems Old and New*. Mervyn Horder, a later Chairman of Duckworth, was also to reissue his novels, including the first, *Before the Bombardment*, which in spite of its limited range he considered a minor classic. In 1952 Horder had the idea of trying to collect all Osbert's short stories into one book, to be published under a joint imprint, Duckworth having originally published two volumes of them, *Triple Fugue* (1924) and *Dumb Animals* (1930), and Macmillan one, *Death of a God* (1949). In the days of a buoyant public library market, this was not a bad plan. Horder later recalled that

> This, I was assured by Osbert's agent David Higham, was an utter impossibility: Macmillan had never done anything under a joint imprint with anyone except once in the war when they had teamed up with O.U.P. for a large printing of *War and Peace*. Higham was wrong, as I fear he often was. I went to see Harold Macmillan, then still head of his firm, and fixed the whole thing with him in five minutes: Osbert Sitwell's *Collected Short Stories* appeared under the joint imprint in 1953 in an edition of 5,000 copies. Not only did Macmillan never bill us for our share of the production expenses, but they delayed all accounting until there was a sizeable profit to send us; they sold out the 5,000 copies, reprinted, and when the sale later fell off made us a present of the remaining stock and their rights in the

book as a whole. Publishers are not all the aggressive cut-throats they are sometimes supposed to be.

For Sachie, Duckworth published *All Summer in a Day* (1926), *The Gothic North*, (1929), and *Dr. Donne and Gargantua* (1930). With powerful encouragement from his sister Edith, and from the rave reviews by the leading critics of the day, Sachie's confidence increased. T.S. Eliot referred to his 'unusual poetic merit'; Arthur Waley, of *170 Chinese Poems* fame, wrote and told him, 'I feel you are certainly the best poet in England', and the *Times Literary Supplement* credited him with 'a radiance and lightness that suggest a joy akin to Shelley's'. Heady stuff, but whether altogether beneficial must be doubted. Of his first prose work, *Southern Baroque Art*, Kenneth Clark later wrote that at the time of its publication 'Baroque and rococo were still terms of abuse ... but such was the sureness of the author's eye, and the persuasive eloquence of his prose, that he created a revolution in the history of English taste.' Osbert, who observed that 'after the Grenadiers you never get used to not being saluted', also later admitted his own 'diseased egotism', and was enormously dependent on Sachie and his devoted brotherly love. However, on Sachie's marriage in 1925 the united front of the trio began to crumble, though their subsequent problems fall outside the scope of this book. Earlier, at the beginning of their crusade against the philistines, Aldous Huxley wrote a rather surprising tribute to them in a letter to his brother Julian: 'They are so earnest and humble ... these dear solid people who have suddenly discovered intellect and got drunk on it.' 'Humble' and 'solid' were not epithets that can ever have been applied to any of them again.

Edith Sitwell, photographed by Cecil Beaton.

Sachie, who was in some ways the most original of the three, was always shy and incurably romantic; hence his utter devotion to Osbert, and later his intense, though conflicting loyalty to his wife Georgia, in spite of her affairs with other men and her uncompromising unwillingness to be swallowed up in the Sitwell mystique. Sachie's mind was like an aviary, which released in rapid succession fascinating flights of information like exotic birds, vanishing rather rapidly over the horizon. He had a great talent for describing the minutiae of physical sensation: sensation, not sense, was his forte; feeling, not thinking; and dream sequences rather than reality. In his travel works, which purported to be historical descriptions of Spain, Portugal and Southern Italy, he was guilty of a gross neglect of the facts. There were no maps in these books, which were poetic-aesthetic ego-trips, and certainly not guide books, except to the contents of his own mind. His instinct was for the beautiful and the odd. His childlike irresponsibility (not least over money) was never cured by any kind of discipline; hence his all-embracing campaign for young ideas, free verse, and modern art of just about any kind, in reaction to the older generation and 'their' war.

To turn to Edith, much evidence has survived, in a long series of letters written by her to Balston between 1924 and his eventual departure from the firm ten years later, that he had a quite exceptional gift as an editor, and in her case as much more than an editor, a real source of support and help in a sometimes lonely life, often beset with hostile attacks. He understood, encouraged and when necessary calmed her down in a way in which it is difficult to imagine anyone else doing with equal success. In return she addressed him, in the dedication of one of her poems, as 'best of friends and most patient of publishers', was constantly asking him to tea in her Bayswater flat, and being asked back to numerous dinners and parties in return.

Edith spent much of her time in Paris during this period, and regularly urged him to come over and meet her friends, such as Gertrude Stein, Pawel Tchelitchew, with whom she was unavailingly in love for a time, and Marie Laurencin, another gifted painter on a minor scale. She also confided in him how she was pestered by Ada Leverson, the faithful friend of Oscar Wilde in his darkest hour, and nicknamed by him the Sphinx. Now, twenty years later, she had evidently become a bit of a bore, and in one letter Edith suddenly breaks into an imaginary monologue addressed by the Sphinx to Moses: 'Darling Moses, aren't you fond of me any more ... Do stop bothering about the Commandments and give it up and come and spend all the rest of your life being smothered by my conversation and marvellous feather boa.' Inconsequential though this is, it somehow gives a stronger impression of what the Sphinx must have been like than would be conveyed by many weary pages of solemn biography. And later, in August 1930, on a visit to Renishaw, the Sitwell family home in Derbyshire, Edith wrote to Balston: 'The Sphinx is here, and very full of girlish questions (she and Reresby [then aged three] vie with each other in their inquiries). When she talks to me, I feel I am being eaten alive by clothes-moths – it isn't a sharp nibbling, like mice – it is a dusty fraying away.' This is Edith at her most acute, but happily Duckworth published, half a century later, a novel by the Sphinx's grandson, the perceptive critic Francis Wyndham.

In typically bizarre fashion, Edith spent Christmas of 1927

in the Curzon Hotel in London, where she fell in with the family of a Parsee dignitary. ('Nobody but me would discover the children of the High Priest of Bombay in a London Hotel on Christmas Day', as she put it ruefully.) She records their conversation as follows: ' "What do *you* think about the New English Prayer Book, Miss Sitwell? Naturally *we* are very interested, as our father is the High Priest of Bombay ... Are you the famous actress, Miss Sitwell? We have seen your portrait." (I think they must have mixed me up with Mrs. Siddons.) "We know all Bombay Society." Oh, I did enjoy it.'

Less enjoyable was her mother's attitude.

> And now Mother is trying to kick up a fresh row. Osbert and I are both in trouble with her. But she never dreams of writing to Osbert, as his nerves mustn't be upset. It doesn't matter about me, as I've only got to earn money, look after Mrs. Powell and Helen, and when not doing this, write poetry. It makes me so cross I could really hit her. Of course it's not poor Osbert's fault; he is an angel of goodness to me, and would give her blazes if he knew. But this attitude of 'Osbert's nerves mustn't be upset', 'Sachie's nerves mustn't be upset', 'Georgia's nerves mustn't be upset' – and that it doesn't matter two hoots about mine, irritates me. Or is beginning to.

But she was always ready to cheer up when circumstances permitted, as on an apparently agreeable sojourn in the Quorn Hall Hotel, Bournemouth, in the following April, where the landlady

> has just told me a long story about how she was bitten by a flea in a hotel at Brighton, when she was fourteen. (She is now sixty-seven.) 'But my dear, you will find nothing of that kind *here*', she assured me. 'For we do not encourage the class of visitor who *walks on the sands*.' Such a good social distinction.

Also of interest is a letter of 1929, when she refers to an attack on her work in the *Daily Mail*, and to a rather unexpected ally: 'Did you see it, and that Bernard Shaw, with the greatest and most airy grace, squashed my opponents absolutely flat. I do think it was sweet of him.' After Christmas she wrote to Balston 'My very best wishes for a very happy New Year. You are one of the very few people who deserve it. You really do.'

As her fame grew, she was approached with commissions to write prose. A few months later, she wrote to Balston that she had been thinking over

> the plan Messrs. Faber suggested for a book on Bath ... I can't afford to refuse their offer of 400 down on advance of royalties ... As you know, I write *prose* simply to make money. Naturally, after your great kindness to me, I should never dream of giving my poetry to any other Publisher but you.

The Sitwells' rapid rise to fame had led to resentment and mockery. Wyndham Lewis, a horse of a very different colour, satirised them in *The Apes of God* as Lord Osmund, Lord Phoebus and Lady Harriet Finnian Shaw, but no less a figure than W.B. Yeats reproached him as follows:

> Somebody tells me that you have satirised Edith Sitwell.

> If that is so, visionary excitement has in part benumbed your senses. When I read her *Gold Coast Customs* a year ago, I felt, as on first reading *The Apes of God*, that something absent from all literature for a generation was back again, and in a form rare in the literature of all generations, passion ennobled by intensity, by endurance, by wisdom.

Coming from one who is agreed generally to be one of the greatest poets of the twentieth century, this is a tribute worth having. But more directly relevant to the history of Duckworth is Edith's reference to the nervous collapse of Mr. Child, the company accountant, presumably brought on by the financial crisis, actual or impending, that was in the air: 'I would have loved to have seen Mr. Duckworth helping to deal with the Crisis, because he always looks gently surprised, and the Crisis would have been enough to astonish anyone ... Poor old man, how frightfully sad and distressing .... Is there really very little chance of his recovering? It is dreadful. I knew him slightly, but only very slightly.'

By a curious chance, another account of this bizarre episode has survived in a letter from Balston to Edith's brother Osbert:

> Our cashier, Child, had been getting odder and odder. Yesterday he locked himself up in the W.C. for an hour and talked loudly to himself, partly like a cat Miaouw – Miaouw, partly foul language. When he was got out, he was obviously quite unaware of what he'd been doing. His work, too, became very odd, and we got into touch with the old ladies who share his house. They had a harrowing story to tell, how he'd been going on like this all night, how he smuggled drugs and drinks in, etc., etc. Arrangements were then made for him to go into a home for 3 months. This morning one of the old ladies, having locked him up and taken his clothes away, came to see us. While she was here, he suddenly arrived (he had found his clothes but not his hat) and went straight to his room as if nothing had happened.

However, the story ends here, and nothing more is recorded of the unfortunate Mr. Child.

In 1933, Edith was awarded the Silver Medal of the Royal Society of Literature, and her father, when informed, 'gave a hollow owl-like hoot of laughter, and said there were far too many poets nowadays. I quite agree.' He and Lady Ida called on their daughter in Paris, and she described their visit to Balston as follows:

> Her ladyship whined and grizzled, and the Baronet sat shaking his head from side to side, not speaking, and trying to convey the impression that he is breaking fast. I should turn giddy if I shook my head like that, so he must be fairly well or he couldn't do it. I had intended not to see the dear old Gentleman, but was trapped into it. When I think of other people being bereaved of their parents, I nearly die of envy.

Back at the office, another crisis overtook Milsted in April 1934. Edith's reaction was one of concern and strong sympathy, and shows how thoughtful and sensitive she could be, especially when not having to contend with her parents.

> Poor Mr. Milsted, I can't tell you how deeply sorry I am

> that he has had to have this new operation. Poor man, I do feel for him, for I have seen so much of these horrors. I do *hope* he is going on well. Do you think, when he is better, I might write him a line of sympathy? I won't till he is better, because it is tiresome for anyone so ill to get letters from people they don't know very well.

Milsted recovered, and soldiered on until after the war, but sadly, Edith's professional relations with Balston soon came to an end, when he gave her the news, shattering to her as well as to him, that he was leaving the firm, as her reaction in July shows:

> I cannot tell you what a frightful shock it has been – actually I simply can't believe it, and only hope you will be able to reconsider it. Nothing will *ever* be the same for us, if we don't have you there. It was you who *made* the place, it was you whom everyone wanted to work for. And to have a great friend who was at the same time in our working life, made all the difference to that working life. I simply can't tell you how frightfully unhappy this has made me, and all the more so because I can read between the lines and see that you have been having the hell of a time. Oh dear! I do *wish* you could tell me what happened, for I shan't know a minute's peace until I do know. But I suppose that is selfish.

There is then a break in the correspondence until December 1935, after Balston had been through some kind of nervous breakdown, and had switched his attention to painting. Edith then wrote as follows, in the last of her letters to him that survives.

> I am most terribly sorry to hear from Osbert that you haven't been at all well, and I do *hope* that you are better, now that you have been able to rest, and are not bothered by Mr. D's intolerable conduct. I am more shocked than I can say by the way he has behaved. And I can just imagine (having suffered from it domestically) the nerve-strain you must have suffered *every* day at lunchtime, knowing what you have to put up with afterwards. The difference in that place since you left is beyond words. I *can't tell* you how terribly I for one, miss you ... naturally, it is needless to say, as a great friend so that it isn't the same coming to the office. But I also miss you terribly from a book-producing point of view, and feel quite helpless without you. Dear good Mr. Lewis does his very best, but it is a Boy-on-the-Burning Deck sort of affair.

The only other letter of interest from Edith Sitwell that has survived was written two months later. A disagreement had arisen with the firm of B.H. Blackwell, which considered that it had acquired the rights in a few of her poems which they had reprinted, probably in an anthology. She wrote a famous letter to Duckworth:

> I have *never* heard anything to exceed Mr. Blackwell's impudence. To my certain knowledge, Osbert bought up all existent copies of 'The Mother', a book for the publication of which I paid. If Mr. Blackwell likes to sue *me* for infringement of copyright he can do so (unless, of course, it means hundreds of pounds). I imagine Mr. Blackwell will be unlikely to stand up to us. Tell him, please, to go to Hell.

If Gerald had had more adventurous and wider tastes, many

Evelyn Waugh by Henry Lamb, 1928.

of the other better young writers of the day, such as Powell's friend Henry Green, might have been scooped up into the Duckworth net. But then he would not have been Gerald. As it was, the firm could well have done worse in the twenties. One of Powell's good ideas was to reissue the out-of-print novels of Ronald Firbank, who had died in 1926, and around whom a stylish myth had grown up. Although he is now largely forgotten except by determined excavators of that decade, he did enjoy a brief re-emergence when one of his novels, *Valmouth* (with some other material added in from another, called *Concerning the Eccentricities of Cardinal Pirelli*) was turned into a successful musical by Sandy Wilson in 1959. Firbank, a notoriously shy man, had in fact left a sum in his will to guarantee the cost of republication. At first, a collected limited edition of a hundred copies, elegantly produced, was issued in 1928, but to everyone's surprise, pre-publication orders came to more than twice that number, and there were several subsequent reprintings of most of his novels. The best of them, in Powell's view, was *Caprice*, which had first been issued, at the author's expense and with a frontispiece by Augustus John, in 1917. *The Flower Beneath the Foot* was first published in 1923, with a decoration by the gifted artist C.R.W. Nevinson, and portraits by John and also Wyndham Lewis. The first of Firbank's books to be accepted without subsidy was *Prancing Nigger*, as it was called in America, though it came out in England under the author's original, and preferred, title, *Sorrow in Sunlight*. Although most of Firbank's novels today seem arbitrary in content, and intolerably precious in style, his dialogue influenced two novelists as different as Ivy Compton Burnett and Evelyn Waugh. Indeed, Waugh later admitted in an interview in 1963 that he had 'cribbed' the dialogue of his earliest novels from Firbank, and when asked if he still enjoyed his source, added that 'there would be something wrong with an elderly man who could enjoy Firbank'. Needless to say, Firbank had become deeply unfashionable in the mood of social concern that followed the slump and the rise of the dictators in Europe, and when the war came, his books were hardly the stuff to stiffen the sinews, let alone to give the troops. Nevertheless, the reissue was an enterprising idea of Powell's, and the *marrons glacés* of Firbank made a pleasing contrast to the steak and kidney pie of Galsworthy.

Powell himself played no part in attaching the Sitwells to Duckworth, since that had already been achieved by Balston before Powell arrived on the scene, but he became friendly with all three of them. His greatest catch, though soon to slip away, was Evelyn Waugh, who without actually misrepresenting his earlier life, afterwards described it with all the artistry one would expect. In the same interview in the *Paris Review* quoted earlier, he gave the following account of his first published book, following a career as a schoolmaster which had somehow lasted for two years.

> After I had been expelled from the second school for drunkenness I returned penniless to my father. I went to see my friend Anthony Powell ... said 'I'm starving.' (This wasn't true: my father fed me.) The director of the firm agreed to pay me £50 for a brief life of Rossetti. I was delighted as fifty pounds was quite a lot then. I dashed off and dashed it off. The result was hurried and bad. I haven't let them reprint it again. Then I wrote *Decline and Fall.*

Gerald vetoed the novel. Waugh had married, in clandestine

fashion, Evelyn Gardner, whose mother's sister was married to Gerald's brother George. There was consequently already heavy disapproval in the air, and in those more innocent days it was quite possible to consider *Decline and Fall* too risqué for a firm as conservative as Duckworth. Balston did his best to save the situation, and keep Waugh on the list, by making suggestions about toning down the passages regarded as offensive. Waugh rejected these and took the book to Chapman & Hall, where his father had been managing director for many years, but was fortunately on holiday at the time, so any embarrassment was avoided. Very minor alterations were again asked for, not much different from those requested by Balston, and this time Waugh agreed to them, perhaps out of relief at not having to deal with a hostile Gerald, and a desire to get the book into print. The compromise reached was that Chapman & Hall should thereafter publish Waugh's novels, but Duckworth should continue with his travel writing. *Labels* (1930), *Remote People* (1931) and *Ninety-Two Days* (1934) were the result. After the war, Waugh collected what he described as 'all that I wish to preserve' of these three volumes, and Duckworth published the result under the title *When the Going was Good*. Another, even more intrepid traveller, Peter Fleming, wrote in a review that 'the more fantastic his predicaments, the more bizarre his encounters, the better Mr. Waugh describes them ... The going is extremely good.' So, for Duckworth, and for the time being, all was not lost. But had it not been for Gerald, a goldmine could have been kept.

Yet another element of Duckworth had been represented at Waugh's wedding by Pansy Pakenham, who had until then shared a flat with the bride, and whose younger sister Violet later married Anthony Powell. *August*, the second of her two novels, was published by the firm in 1931, blazing a trail for what was to become the vast literary output of her large family for the rest of the century. *August*, though almost unprocurable today, is a fascinating period piece, well worth reading. It is based on the world into which she had been introduced by her considerably older husband, the painter Henry Lamb, whose portraits of Lytton Strachey and Evelyn Waugh are deservedly well known. He had been at the hub of the world of Garsington, presided over by Lady Ottoline Morrell, and well brought to life in her biography by Sandra Jobson Darroch. It included at one time or another such luminaries as D.H. Lawrence, Bertrand Russell, Siegfried Sassoon, T.S. Eliot, Katharine Mansfield, and the painters Mark Gertler and Duncan Grant. The novel contains echoes of Aldous Huxley, another habitué of Garsington, and contains some rather barbed generalisations in the manner later mastered by Ivy Compton Burnett. Surprisingly, Pansy Pakenham made the narrator of *August* a man, and the result is a livelier treatment of the milieu which was later to be described in flatter tones, after the slump, by her future brother-in-law in his *Dance to the Music of Time*. Two brief samples give some idea of its flavour, and the second is an admirable description of Garsington life.

> Clare was sufficiently a good friend of everybody to secure confidences, but not so good a friend as to keep them ....

> In what did they [i.e. the Garsington Brigade] differ from other people except in a complacent belief that they were different, and in fear of losing their intellectual purity? Obsessed with this terror they huddled together in a fortified monastery, where, safe from the gross assaults of the outside world, they could nevertheless chastise it with

Gerald Duckworth and Queen Marie of Roumania on the steps of the Garrick Club.

sharp arrows shot from commanding loopholes. True, within these bounds, high standards of cultivation were maintained, a delightful sense of intimacy prevailed, and the cruder forms of charlatanism were unknown.

Sadly, Gerald prevented Balston from establishing himself more fruitfully in this promised land, where some of the most successful and interesting of the writers of the twenties were of course to be found. A pent-up feeling of frustration at this denial was to be one of the chief reasons for the rift that would later drive the unfortunate Balston from the Duckworth fold.

Powell had other disappointments over authors he recommended at the time, though every publisher would admit to similar misjudgments. Duckworth turned down Antonia White's *Frost in May*, which has been in print ever since; also Christopher Isherwood's *The Memorial*, and *Miss Lonelyhearts* by Nathanael West; but the fact that they were offered to the firm gives an idea of the leading position it held. Powell did however get a revised version of Wyndham Lewis's *Tarr* accepted in 1928. Other authors of interest were Queen Marie of Roumania, whose first novel *The Voice on the Mountain* appeared in 1924. A remarkable photograph is reproduced here showing Gerald and the Queen emerging from the Garrick Club, probably after a good lunch and certainly after a game of bridge, in which he and Balston and what looks like a lady in waiting made up the four. Oral tradition relates that at some point the Queen's pearl necklace became unstrung, and Gerald and Balston were observed on their hands and knees, dutifully hunting for the pearls which had been scattered over the carpet.

Also in 1928, Balston took on the first book by the twenty-three-year-old Robert Byron, *The Station*, which was resurrected twenty-five years later under the imprint of John Lehmann. Byron was a contemporary of Waugh and Powell, though both had their reservations about him. He was to become, with David Talbot Rice, the leading expert on Byzantine art and architecture, till then the preserve of strict academics who had no interest in popularising their subject. But Robert Byron's energy, enthusiasm and appetite for arduous travel brought the subject within the range of the general reader, though Balston was often 'begging him apprehensively not to make it too serious'. Byron was certainly not lacking in self-confidence. But there is something to say the least unreasonable about the letter that he wrote to his mother complaining that 'the cover of the book is to be *hideous* – but I can struggle with Duckworth's incompetence no more. It is going to be plain royal blue – I can't help it – it is the only good colour that they can offer – and I will not have a bad colour, so there is an end of it.' This bears out Powell's observation that authors cared more about the details of the presentation of their work than they are able to do today. Happily, a month later, Byron reported that 'Duckworth's are taking a most tremendous lot of trouble with advertising, circulars, etc.'

At Evelyn Waugh's first wedding Byron for some reason gave the bride away, perhaps because, given the clandestine circumstances, there was no one else to hand. Another letter from Byron to his mother gives an idea of the mood in which this marriage was embarked on, and, no doubt, of why it could later be annulled. 'These weddings! It really is too awful – I have to *fetch* Evelyn Gardner to the church and I know she won't come.' He was also in the habit of giving prolonged imitations of Queen Victoria, both in appearance and in what he considered to be her manner of speech. Like her, Gerald would not have been amused, but probably they were never allowed by Balston to meet. Byron's collected letters to his mother, well edited by his sister Lucy Butler, were published in 1991. They are full of life and fun, but as he was obliged to earn his living by high-class, poorly paid journalism, his contribution to the Duckworth list was sadly restricted, and his next book, *The Byzantine Experience*, was published by Routledge. James Lees-Milne, whose huge literary success was to follow half a century later, was at this time a close friend of Byron's and his description of him in *Fourteen Portraits* (1996) is of more than passing interest, since in many ways he epitomised the bright, and often angry and rude, young men of the twenties and thirties, who while not being deceived into supporting communism, nevertheless clamoured more or less blindly for a break with the world of their parents' generation.

Byron's father seems to have been mild and unremarkable. His mother however was robust and matter of fact by nature. She adored her son, was passionately interested in his ideas, and to some degree receptive of them, and gave him every encouragement within her means, in spite of the often raffish, cynical nature of his circle of friends. Byron played a leading part in the vigorous literary and social milieu of the day, or at least in the public-school element in it. Henry Yorke (Green), Evelyn Waugh himself, Christopher Sykes, Alan Pryce-Jones, Harold Acton were all at one time or another his close friends, and towards the end of her life Nancy Mitford was to refer to him as 'perhaps the dead person I miss most'. As an undergraduate in that much described circle, he became passionately interested in architecture, and as Lees-Milne records, 'before he was twenty-one he knew his mission in life exactly: to be the historian of Byzantine civilisation through the medium of painting and architecture'; that is to say, not by acquiring real scholarship in that field, but through first-hand observation, sometimes in company with friends much richer than himself; though at that time, however rich you were, travel in Greece and Turkey was infinitely more uncomfortable and difficult than it is for the most penurious back-packer today. Boisterous wit and infectious enthusiasm were his substitutes for learning, and explain the success of his books. His first, *The Station*, was a rather unhelpfully titled description of Mount Athos. It pays homage to Byzantine Greece, while railing at its modern descendants, in a richly deserved way, for so criminally neglecting and ignoring their cultural inheritance, and being quite unashamed of his own frankly admitted complete lack of ordinary good manners towards his dilatory hosts. Some of his prejudices were fatuous: in his besotted eyes, there was no merit of any kind in Shakespeare, Rembrandt or the Christian Church. But his sheer enthusiasm, anyway in small doses, was evidently irresistible. Lees-Milne quotes a passage from *The Station* which I make no apology for repeating here:

> Let him who still conceives of Byzantine painting as a hieratic degradation, imagine a Giotto unsweetened, as Giotto already was, by Italianate naturalism, painting in the luminous colours of El Greco – those cold blues and clarets, olive-shadowed yellows, and pure, clear green of under the sea; lit with angry brilliance; geometric in form, yet in austerity sympathetic, in power gentle. It is these, the very flower of the Byzantine Renaissance – not only the link between European art and the East, final explication of El Greco, but in themselves divorce from history, masterpieces of the world, that are threatened by neglect. These were the treasures that should be preserved and cherished in their rightful setting, instead of being allowed to rot through lack of interest, funds and expertise in caring for them.

But what greatly increases Byron's significance in the contemporary scene is that by the middle 1930s he had moved from Byzantium to far more urgent general horrors at home. In a vibrant pamphlet, *How We Celebrate the Coronation Year* (1937), decades ahead of the field, he laid into unscrupulous property developers, not least the Church Commissioners, whose philistine vandalism goes back even beyond that time, for demolishing classical streets and Wren churches four years before Hitler and Goering took over the job themselves. Byron went so far as to describe the Bishop of London as 'this mitred serpent'. But in general political matters his zeal went wider and stronger still. He became President of something called the Federal Union Club, even further ahead of its time, in that it encouraged the democracies of Europe to form a kind of loose federation in order to halt the landslide into Nazi and Fascist tyranny. The fact that none of the relevant countries was remotely prepared to do so did not deter Byron for a second, and it is impossible not to respect and admire his insular vision of a means of salvation from the thugs and brigands who were so soon to bring about the war.

Two anecdotes confirm his courage and his patriotism. When appeasement of Hitler was at its height, with *The Times* in the forefront, Byron caused a mild sensation at the crowded lunch table at the Beefsteak Club by loudly asking the Editor, Geoffrey Dawson, 'Are you in German pay?' As it happened, a similar question was asked by Léon Blum, probably the most intelligent and certainly the most civilised Prime Minister of France between the wars. On a despairing visit to London in 1939, he met Dawson and afterwards inquired, 'Who was that man, *that German*?' Byron also observed to Chips Channon, the anglicised American millionaire Conservative MP, who was likewise thought to be over-tolerant of the Nazis: 'I see you put the interests of your adopted class before those of your adopted country', a remark which not surprisingly remained unrecorded in the Channon diaries. Thanks to his intimate knowledge of Persia, Byron was given an intelligence job in the war, and was sent to Meshed to keep an eye on the activities of the Russians in the area. His cover was to proceed first to Cairo as war correspondent of the *Sunday Times*, with the blessing of its proprietor Lord Kemsley. But the small ship on which he set out was torpedoed by the *Scharnhorst* off the north coast of Scotland, and he was 'lost at sea by enemy action'. All accounts of him elsewhere, together with his delightful letters to his mother, indicate that he was one of the most attractive and colourful, if unpredictable and sometimes plain intolerable characters to have featured on the Duckworth list either before or since.

Another introduction by Powell about that time was Roger Fulford, a gifted biographer, generally of eighteenth-century royalty, then very much out of fashion. *Royal Dukes* (1933) and *George IV*, a Book Society choice in 1934, were his first successes. Though his style of biography was later overtaken in popularity by a more thorough and detailed approach, he succeeded in catching the spirit of an age with skill and sympathy, and his books can still be enjoyed today. The sporting side of the list, perhaps fostered by Milsted, was kept up by the well known golfer Henry Longhurst, who (jointly with Charles Graves) produced *Candid Caddies*, and also by Bernard Darwin with *W.G. Grace* in the Great Lives series. This series of short biographies, published at two shillings a copy, was another worthwhile venture of Balston's. Subjects ranged in time from *Alfred the Great* to *T.E. Lawrence*, in subject from *Spinoza* to *Handel*. Well known contributors included Rose Macaulay on Milton, Bernard Darwin on Dickens as well as on W.G. Grace, Peter Quennell on Byron, and Gerald Abraham on Nietzsche and Dostoievsky. Many were reprinted, and after the war a new style of wrapper was designed for them by John Piper. It was the kind of bread-and-butter business on which a small firm can keep alive, and it served its purpose well.

Back in 1925, Duckworth had also published a fairly obscure academic book which had interesting repercussions. *Mystery Cities & Exploration and Adventures in Lubaantun* by Thomas Gann aroused the interest of T.A. Joyce, Deputy Keeper of Ceramics and Ethnography at the British Museum. In the following year Gann led the first British Museum Expedition to British Honduras, which was to make important archaeological and ethnographical discoveries.

THE NEW READERS' LIBRARY.

Printed on thin paper, and bound in flexible cloth. Size 7 × 4½ in. Price 3s. 6d. each.

A new series of important copyright works by eminent modern authors many of which have never before been available at standard prices. The volumes, which are uniform in size, binding and price, have been specially designed with the assistance of an expert printer and binder, to meet the modern demand for handier books, without sacrifice of the dignity and simplicity which are essential to a good appearance on the shelves of a Library. Among the authors whose works are included in the first lists are—

Maurice Baring
Hilaire Belloc
Augustine Birrell
Edmund Blunden
David W. Bone
William Gerhardi
Michael Fairless
W. H. Hudson
Richard Jefferies
Edith Sitwell
Osbert Sitwell
Sacheverell Sitwell
Anton Tchekoff
H. M. Tomlinson
R. B. Cunninghame Graham

and arrangements are now being made for the inclusion of many other works of equal value.

It will be noted that, while all the volumes are of high literary standing, the Library is peculiarly rich in the literature of the open-air, including such famous books as W. H. Hudson's "Green Mansions" and "Birds and Man," H. M. Tomlinson's "The Sea and the Jungle," Michael Fairless's "The Roadmender," Edmund Blunden's "The Bonadventure" (a unique and too little known travel book written in a modern spirit) and David Bone's sea yarn "The Brassbounder." The same note is struck by such novels as Hudson's "The Purple Land" and Richard Jefferies "Amaryllis at the Fair."

THE SLUMP AND THE WAR
1932-1945

Long before Allen Lane launched Penguin, vigorous attempts had been made by leading publishers to reach the mass markets which had been created by the spread of popular education. The earliest and biggest of these had been the two World Classics series issued by both Collins and Nelson in Scotland in 1907. Duckworth had eventually followed suit in a small way and by 1931 the New Readers' Library contained forty-four titles. The advertisement which was printed at the end of every copy of each book is reproduced opposite. It gives a flavour of the stately tone in which customers were addressed at the time.

Nevertheless, the slump was as unkind to publishers as it was to everyone else. The minute book records no dividends after the bumper year of 1931, and in 1932 the director's fees were reduced by half, and Powell's salary by £200. By that time, relations between Gerald and Balston had plainly sunk to an all-time low, partly, according to Powell, because of Gerald's pent-up rage on the subject of the Sitwells, Waugh 'and other modern abominations' introduced by Balston; partly also, perhaps, by the suggestion of a further cut in directors' fees. At a heated board meeting on 18 August 1934, Milsted loyally, but probably not out of true sympathy, cast his vote with Gerald, and Balston had no option but to resign his directorship. He had served Duckworth, again in Powell's words, 'not without a degree of distinction and individuality' for a dozen years. In consequence of this disaster, he suffered a nervous breakdown and did not feel able to pursue his career in another firm. There is a bitter irony in the fact that if this crisis could have been postponed by two years, Gerald would have been dead and Balston would almost certainly have taken his place.But as it was, he may well have felt to some degree let down by Milsted, and after a long visit to Spain he took up painting and also later wrote one or two more books himself, and when the second war came served briefly as a staff officer. After Gerald had moved on to the Great Clubhouse in the Sky, Balston took to haunting the Garrick, and to harping on the subject of how *Decline and Fall* had slipped through his fingers to anyone who would listen. A melancholy end, which publishers should take care to avoid. He survived into his mid-eighties, an achievement less common then than now. Ironically, he had been taken on originally as a partner by Gerald in 1926 because Milsted was thought to be terminally ill. As it turned out, Milsted outlasted Balston in the firm by over twenty years, and saw it through the second war in the absence of the younger directors who had joined the forces.

Balston had for some time been hinting that Powell's own place in the firm was insecure, but Powell himself modestly records that 'Gerald's preference for making no change whatever in any circumstances included by this time a lack of any active inclination to get rid of me; and in any case editorial and other odd jobs had to be done by someone'.

THE NEW READERS LIBRARY

*

1. GREEN MANSIONS by W. H. HUDSON
2. THE POLYGLOTS by WILLIAM GERHARDI
3. THE SEA AND THE JUNGLE by H. M. TOMLINSON
4. THE ROADMENDER by MICHAEL FAIRLESS
5. THE TERROR by ARTHUR MACHEN
6. LOST DIARIES by MAURICE BARING
7. THE BONADVENTURE by EDMUND BLUNDEN
8. SUCCESS by CUNNINGHAME GRAHAM
9. BIRDS AND MAN by W. H. HUDSON
10. THE BLACK MONK by ANTON TCHEKOFF
11. GOD'S COUNTRY by JAMES OLIVER CURWOOD
12. BUCOLIC COMEDIES by EDITH SITWELL
13. THE BRASSBOUNDER by DAVID W. BONE
14. THE PURPLE LAND by W. H. HUDSON
15. CALIBAN'S GUIDE TO LETTERS AND LAMBKIN'S REMAINS by HILAIRE BELLOC
16. OBITER DICTA by AUGUSTINE BIRRELL
17. AMARYLLIS AT THE FAIR by RICHARD JEFFERIES
18. A CRYSTAL AGE by W. H. HUDSON
19. THE KISS by ANTON TCHEKOFF
20. GOSSIP OF THE 17TH AND 18TH CENTURIES by JOHN BERESFORD
21. FUTILITY by WILLIAM GERHARDI
22. TRIPLE FUGUE by OSBERT SITWELL
23. EL OMBU by W. H. HUDSON
24. SIX SHORT PLAYS by JOHN GALSWORTHY
25. ARGONAUT AND JUGGERNAUT by OSBERT SITWELL
26. SOCIAL LIFE IN THE INSECT WORLD by J. H. FABRE
27. WONDERS OF INSTINCT by J. H. FABRE
28. ENGLISH LITERATURE AND SOCIETY IN THE 18TH CENTURY by SIR LESLIE STEPHEN
29. IN THE FOREIGN LEGION by LÉGIONNAIRE 17889
30. HAMPSHIRE DAYS by W. H. HUDSON
31. THE SHEPHERD by EDMUND BLUNDEN
32. ANTON CHEKOV by WILLIAM GERHARDI
33. BIRDS IN LONDON by W. H. HUDSON
34. THIRTEEN STORIES by CUNNINGHAME GRAHAM
35. THE MEANING OF DEMOCRACY by IVOR BROWN
36. WILD NATURE'S WAYS by RICHARD KEARTON
37. THE ART OF LETTERS by ROBERT LYND
38. TWENTY-SIX MEN AND A GIRL by MAXIM GORKY
39. ENGLISH POEMS by EDMUND BLUNDEN
40. THE GATHERING OF BROTHER HILARIUS by MICHAEL FAIRLESS
41. HIGH TIDE by MRS. WALDO RICHARDS
42. FAITH by R. B. CUNNINGHAME GRAHAM
43. THE HUNDRED AND ONE HARLEQUINS by SACHEVERELL SITWELL
44. SCOTTISH STORIES by R. B. CUNNINGHAME GRAHAM

Thus did Powell survive. However, Balston had been Powell's chief ally and fellow spirit in the firm, and Powell soon began to look elsewhere for an occupation which would support him in married life, while enabling him to continue writing novels. After the war he established himself with the series of novels called *A Dance to the Music of Time*, published by Heinemann, for which a substantial cult was to arise both in England and, more surprisingly, in America. He was eventually made a Companion of Honour, and by long outliving his contemporaries such as Evelyn Waugh and Graham Greene, slowly rose to the position of Grand Old Man of the English Novel. He certainly achieved greater public fame than anyone else who ever worked at Duckworth, greater too than that of nearly all its authors.

Between the arrival of Powell and the departure of Balston, the other principal newcomer to Duckworth was Alan Harris, who joined it from the steady, largely academic firm of G. Bell & Sons in 1929, but was not made a director until 1938. He had narrowly missed a fellowship at Balliol, Powell's own college. Balston was apparently against Harris being made a director, but he had become influential as the adviser on scholastic and educational books (though few such were published by the firm at that time), and came to play a more formal part it after the departure of Balston and the death of Gerald. Harris was much liked by Powell and also later by Patrick Crichton-Stuart, another Balliol man who joined the firm after Gerald's death, when he acquired the founder's own shares. Harris was well qualified to maintain high editorial standards, not least in two series that had been instituted by Balston: Great Lives and the Hundred Years Series, for which Harris would find authors, including Gerald Abraham for Music, J.C. Flugel for Psychology and K.B. Smellie for English Government. Harris's wife Angelica was Russian, and an expert pianist, a talent which was to provide a link with Mervyn Horder when he joined the firm in 1938. But she also provided yet another streak of the eccentricity which was seldom absent for long from Duckworth, with her unusual talent for being able to catch flies, in flight, between finger and thumb.

The last board meeting with Gerald in the chair took place on 31 May 1937. Later that year, while on holiday, he was taken ill and died in Milan. His obituary in *The Times* gave him his due as an old-fashioned 'gentleman publisher' and mentioned that apart from the rest of his club life he had been Honorary Secretary of the Savile for many years.

In 1939 Harris left to become a civil servant in the War Office, and after the war was over he was made civil administrator for the Army Military College at Shrivenham, and later for the Royal Hospital at Chelsea. All this time, however, he kept in touch with Duckworth, and contributed introductions to such books as *Eight Famous Plays* by Strindberg, and Firbank's *The New Rythum*, successfully making them accessible to the general reader.

But above all it was A.G. Lewis who, in Mervyn Horder's words, 'did more than anyone to hold the shaky firm together through the ups and downs from 1923 to 1950'. Powell, in his memoirs, gives a detailed description which brings him to life with some precision.

> He belonged firmly to the old fashioned middle class, when the term really had some meaning. No one ... was less prepared than he to move with the times, become assimilated with a contemporary scene in which social differences had begun to become blurred. Lewis would have none of that. He allowed absolutely no adjustment in relations with those he considered above or below him. He knew precisely where he stood, desired nothing else .... He also wore a black coat and striped trousers, the coat fastened in the Victorian manner only by its high top button.
>
> At times irritable, ... Lewis was a very nice man, straightforward, kind-hearted, absolutely reliable. At the same time, he had his limitations, would also bemoan anything taken on that had the air of being highbrow, or required presentation in what he regarded as a highbrow manner. He was Balston's subordinate, but Balston, if not exactly afraid of Lewis, never liked to cross him too far .... Lewis was, quite rightly, always keen on economy in printing and binding ... but moments come when exceptions must be allowed. Authors go to small publishers to get individual attention .... In those days writers thought more than they do now about their work appearing in elegant form. In such matters young and farouche authors could find Lewis, who was painfully shy, difficult to deal with. This might hasten departure to another firm.

As 'manager' Lewis was responsible for all the day-to-day running of the business: producing and storing the books, being in charge of the sales department, appointing staff and sales representatives, looking after export business, and supervising accounts and authors' royalties. He had accompanied Balston from Fisher Unwin, and had actually entered that firm a few weeks earlier than the great Stanley

Unwin, who was later to found the very successful if austere firm of Allen & Unwin, and to be knighted for services to the book trade which in the eyes of others besides himself were of a very high order. Lewis, never one to be overawed, later observed to Horder sardonically, 'Yes, I was the one who taught Stanley Unwin most of whatever he knows.' Lewis survived the publishing doldrums of the late 1930s, before and after Gerald's death, and for the whole of the Second World War. It was not until 1948, long overdue for retirement, that he decided to go, and Horder, who was by then chairman, replaced him with a former colleague of his at Methuen, Charles Walton.

But perhaps Lewis's greatest service to the firm, according to Horder, was a hidden one. When Horder and Crichton-Stuart arrived on the scene in 1938, it was not disclosed to them that Duckworth owed the book-binders Key & Whiting £11,000 (perhaps £300,000 in today's money). It was Stanley Unwin, who was a director of Key & Whiting, who, in Horder's words, 'made them stay their hand, with words to the effect that "My friend A.G. Lewis is manager of that firm, and he'll see you get your money in the end." When the war came, and more or less every book sold, they did.'

1932 however was to be the year of crisis. The property was mortgaged to the bank, to support an increase in the overdraft facility from £4,000 to £6,000. In 1934, things must have looked up again, since Balston's salary went up from £400 to £600. This may have been a sop to his discontent, but if so it was not successful, and on 18 August Balston resigned in disgust, as has been seen, probably as a result of some final clash with Gerald's obscurantist attitudes, though exact details are not available. Curiously enough, Milsted had hardly been paid at all, perhaps because he had spent so little time in the office. But now his salary went up first from £150 to £250, and again, after the departure of Balston, to £500, no doubt reflecting an increased workload. After Gerald's last board meeting on 31 May no further meeting was held till 23 March 1938, when Alan Harris was made a director at a salary of £550. Milsted was formally appointed chairman, and on 20 October Crichton-Stuart and Horder were appointed directors, each at a salary of £450, with Milsted now being paid £750. Horder, who was a keen musician, and later composed settings of various poems, is said to have done little after coming down from Cambridge except to play the piano at home. His father, an eminent physician who had been rewarded with a peerage for his services to three sovereigns, urged him to become a publisher. After the war, his father originated the Modern Health Series for Duckworth. It was welcomed by the *Lancet*, which said that it 'should do a useful or much-needed job'. Doctors of distinction, to whom Horder obviously had easy access, wrote on heart disease, rheumatism, varicose veins, epilepsy, tuberculosis, skin diseases, cancer, childbirth, diabetes and foot troubles. The books ran to about 128 pages and sold in hardback at 8/6, and undoubtedly brought comfort and relief to many sufferers. They were more than once reissued in the 1950s and 60s.

One of Horder's first acts on arriving at the firm was to arrange for all Belloc's comic verse to be issued with the original illustrations, at first by 'B.T.B.' (Lord Basil Blackwood) and after his death in action in 1917, at the age of forty-seven, by Nicholas Bentley, in a single omnibus edition called *Cautionary Verses*, which remained an essential ingredient in British nurseries until the late 1980s. Horder would claim that this not only had the effect of making the Duckworth travellers welcome in every bookshop in the land, but also of inducing Knopf to bring out the verses in America for the first time.

Horder had worked briefly at Methuen and then in the publicity department of Thomas Nelson before joining Duckworth and was thus familiar with their trade organisation, their team of travellers, who numbered seven as against Duckworth's three, and their overseas agencies. In 1939 it was arranged for Nelson to take on the warehousing and distribution of Duckworth's list, a type of arrangement that later became quite common after the war and the rapid inflation of costs of all kinds. It bore further fruit when in December 1940 Nelson's offices in Paternoster Row were flattened in the air raid which also slightly damaged St. Paul's Cathedral nearby. Duckworth was able to offer them office space in Henrietta Street the very next day, presumably in what had been their warehouse until the distribution arrangement with Nelson had been formed. Nelson remained there until 1950, when they moved to Park Street, Mayfair. For about a year, Horder also took on editorial responsibility for the Nelson Classics series on the retirement of John Hampden, but in the summer of 1940 publishing was taken off the list of reserved occupations which absolved those who worked in them from conscription. Horder then joined the RAFVR, in which he served with some distinction for the rest of the war, at first with Fighter Command, where he developed a system of predicting the direction being taken by the German bombers. There is no documentary proof, but the story goes that Churchill gave instructions that Horder was to be made an Air Vice-Marshal in recognition of his work, in order to give it greater significance, but that he declined the promotion on the grounds that it was quite excessive. Later, he served with South-East Asia Command in Colombo; and finally in Tokyo. He reached the rank of wing commander, and was mentioned in despatches.

Among other pieces of curious information which he liked to collect was the fact that when the Duckworth and Nelson books were stored together in the Paternoster Row basement, the local rats showed a distinct preference for Duckworth books. The reason turned out to be that Nelson's bindery in Edinburgh used a deterrent in the form of red squill in the glue used in binding. Duckworth's binders were not up to this canny dodge, and the Duckworth stock suffered accordingly. The city ratcatcher eventually visited the premises and caught over seventy rats in a single night, later describing his work on BBC radio. (There was a happy ending many years later, in December 1995, when Duckworth bought the Thomas Nelson Classics list, itself taken over by Nelson from Macmillan several years previously. The acquisition of key texts such as Stanford's *Odyssey*, Willcock's *Iliad*, Williams's *Aeneid* and Goodwin's *Greek Grammar* assured Duckworth's position as the country's leading publisher of classical set texts and grammars.)

During the war, reading became a great solace to innumerable people who may not have indulged in it to any great extent before, especially those who were trapped amid the dangers of big cities and air raids, with travel and entertainment of any kind heavily curtailed. The poet and editor John Lehmann described it as 'a great feast of reading'. One of the feasts was a poetry reading by Edith Sitwell in a club for allied officers in Westminster run by Pamela Churchill, at that time wife of Randolph Churchill. By this stage in the war, 1944, the earlier general dread of air raids had been replaced by a more specific and acute fear of flying bombs, whose engines cut out before landing and exploding. John Lehmann gave an eye-witness account of the scene after the sinister throb of the approaching buzz bomb could be heard, and the warden had blown his whistle in Dean's Yard outside the windows.

> It was a magnificent performance, worthy of a British admiral coolly dictating orders from the bridge in the middle of a naval engagement. She held the whole audience in the grip of her discipline .... As the bomb came overhead, its engine died and one knew with the relief of experience that its load of death and destruction must glide on beyond the immediate vicinity. Edith still read on, coming finally to her last line:
>
> 'Still do I love, still shed my innocent light, my Blood for thee!'

As she finished, the bomb exploded, perhaps a mile away. There was deafening applause, admiration for her courage mixed with relief that they were all still alive. Later, Edith described the scene herself in a letter to her friend Evelyn Weil:

> The warning went, the chug-chug-chug of the V1 bomb, and the whistle blew. Which is the signal for imminent danger!!! I must say I *did* feel rather old-fashioned, as the thing was just over the roof, where it remained chugging about *throughout* the poem!!! However I continued to read as if nothing was happening, and the thing by a miracle went away. But of course some other poor wretches got it.

It has been suggested that energy and self-assurance rather than talent had sometime been responsible for the Sitwells' success, but that has been true of many other authors before and since. What is certain is that they can never have been guilty of a lack of courage.

A month before the air raid which bombed Nelsons out of Paternoster Row, a similar disaster had occurred at a warehouse in Edmonton where Duckworth's entire stock of unbound sheets, over 400,000 copies of six hundred titles, was destroyed. War damage insurance was only negligible compensation for this shattering loss, and paper restrictions prevented firms which had suffered in this way from making good their losses: for want of a better yardstick, each publisher's quota of paper was based on the amount they had used in the last year before the war. But Milsted and Lewis laboured unflaggingly to keep things going, and ironically one of the more distinguished books to appear on the list in 1940 was *German Lyrics of the 17th Century*, edited by August Closs, later Professor of German at Bristol University, and W.F. Maitland. For sheer escapism during the blitz, a life of Horace Walpole by Wyndham Ketton-Cremer, a learned landowner and historian of Norfolk and of much else, earned high marks, and *Oscar Wilde, A Summing Up*, by Lord Alfred Douglas, considerably lower ones.

St Paul's during the Blitz.

DEFINITIVE THIRD EDITION
PUCCINI
Mosco
Carner

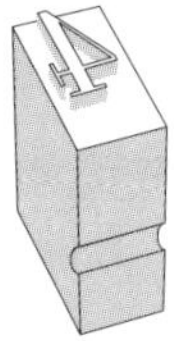

THE DOLDRUM YEARS
1946-1967

There was little or no improvement in general conditions when the war was finally over. Rationing and shortages of all kinds continued, and strikes and power cuts were frequent, and particularly depressing in the two exceptionally hard winters which followed the end of the war. A rare bright spot was the issue in 1946 of *When the Going was Good,* a collection of Evelyn Waugh's travel writing, already mentioned. Two years later, Balston's connection with Duckworth was revived when they published his biography of the wildly imaginative Victorian painter, John Martin, which he dedicated to Edith Sitwell.

Patrick Crichton-Stuart, who had bought Gerald Duckworth's shares from his widow in 1937, returned to the firm in 1946, and in more favourable circumstances might well have picked up the threads of Balston's successful achievement of attracting bright young authors to the Duckworth list. But, perhaps from a shortage of working capital in the firm, this did not happen. Instead, in the age of 'little magazines', he edited, from Henrietta Street, a high-class example of the genre, between eighty and a hundred pages long. It was at first entitled *Galleon,* but later, 'as a result of having been overlooked by some who misunderstood the title', presumably connecting it vaguely with naval history, it was renamed *Choice.* It served as a kind of shop-window for current literature, and consisted of short extracts from forthcoming and recently published books, in the days before serialisation in the Sunday papers had come into fashion. The third *Galleon* contained extracts from a very wide range of interesting and enjoyable titles. Osbert Sitwell on *Brighton Aquatints,* published in 1939; an excellent page and a half from Field Marshal Lord Wavell's *The Good Soldier*; a short story by Chekhov; a strange account by Freya Stark of a club for the descendants of Nubian slaves in Kuwait. There was a good extract from Trotsky's life of Stalin, unfinished at the time of the author's murder in Mexico; and a much less good piece by Sir Paul Dukes from a curiously naïve book about Russia entitled *Come Hammer, Come Sickle,* interesting all the same as an example of the still prevailing misconceptions about our recent ally, already our potential enemy in the Cold War. There was also an extract called 'In Darkest Africa' from Albert Schweitzer's *On the Edge of the Primeval Forest.*

Altogether, it was a selection of which any editor could feel proud. *Choice* had been launched not as a 'pre-digested snack' but as 'the best of current reading and the surest guide to better acquaintance with the authors and their books'. It would be interesting to know what circulation was built up among a new reading public, but sadly no records appear to have survived. The books were to include *The Essence of Modern Conservatism* by Harold Macmillan, and 'Such Wicked Nonsense' by Bernard Shaw, from *Fabian Essays in Socialism,* as well as pieces by Dorothy Sayers,

Desmond Shawe-Taylor on Covent Garden, and Sophie Tucker's *Humble Origins*. However, Crichton-Stuart felt decreasing enthusiasm for the plainly rather subdued mood of the post-war years at Duckworth, and eventually resigned his directorship in 1954. For a time he ran a fruit farm in Hampshire. Later, he pioneered a series of art-historical tours for Cadogan Travel, taking parties of museum directors and others to America as soon as currency restrictions began to be relaxed. This was no doubt a more rewarding experience for someone of his talents than life in the dilapidated office in Henrietta Street, still much as it had been in Anthony Powell's day, but with an extra dinginess added to it by the neglect of the war years and by no means remedied by the arrival of peace. Milsted had finally retired in 1949 after no less than forty-five years with the firm. 3,400 of his shares were acquired by Crichton-Stuart, and 5,150 by Horder. Lewis retired in the same year. Horder's management of the company remained prudent and low-key, and about twenty new books a year were published, following no particular pattern, but selected rather arbitrarily in accordance with Horder's various fancies.

No catalogues were preserved (or survived the eventual move from Henrietta Street) until 1952, after which there is an almost complete series. New books remained scanty, and it was the various series already mentioned that must have provided what bread and butter there was. A new publishing partnership, consisting of James Macgibbon and Robert Kee, was given a rent-free lease of two rooms on the second floor of Henrietta Street, in return for an arrangement for Duckworth to distribute the books. Three years later, Macgibbon and Kee were swallowed up by another group, but had already published some new books of real distinction. James Macgibbon later joined Gollancz, and finally David and Charles, while Robert Kee made a very successful career in television before turning to authorship with such large-scale books as *The Green Flag* and *Ireland: A History*. On Crichton-Stuart's resignation 8,000 of his shares were acquired by C.H.P. Gifford and his wife. Gifford had been at Winchester with Horder, and as an academic economist had become a fellow of Magdalene College, Cambridge, before the war. Later he served in the Ministry of Economic Warfare, then in the Foreign Office until 1949, and next for two years at the United Nations. He then turned his attention to the world of investment trusts, and his involvement with Duckworth was not so much for financial gain as to make use of his academic experience in economics by introducing books in that field for publication. One of the first of these was by his close friend Nicholas Kaldor, a Hungarian who later played a part in the disastrous policies of Harold Wilson. Obviously, Gifford had been moving in much more exalted official circles than anyone previously connected with Duckworth, and the books that he introduced, pedestrian and even unreadable to the layman though they may have been, probably made a modest contribution to the stability of the company. He remained a director until July 1969. 1955 was the year in which the faithful Lewis retired, and was succeeded as Company Secretary by J.J. Murdin. Gifford was appointed a director in July, and a modest bonus scheme was set up for the directors and staff.

Duckworth edged forward, making a profit of £2,523 in 1957 and £1,200 in 1958, and in 1960 it was agreed that Chatto & Windus should acquire 60% of the company and take over trade distribution, the intention also being that Duckworth should move into Chatto's offices in King William Street nearby, at the end of the year. Three of their directors, publishers of considerable distinction but different priorities, Peter Calvocoressi, Norah Smallwood and Piers Raymond, briefly joined the Duckworth board in 1960 but resigned the following year. The Duckworth directors soon came to feel, probably rightly, that their books were being treated as a mere afterthought by the Chatto sales force, and to avoid probable recriminations, the arrangement was discontinued and the move was never made.

As regards the novelties, the menu was extremely varied. It briefly included Simone De Beauvoir, a mistress of Sartre and at that time the *dernier cri* of existentialism. The book, *America Day by Day*, was the diary of a recent tour. Years later, in 1979, Duckworth received an inquiry from a large contractor for school supplies, and general bookseller, asking if *America Day by Day* was going to be reprinted in view of the large sales of the author's other books in paperback. The chilly answer came back that the book 'had been remaindered, is now very much out of date and we do not intend to reprint it'. It contrasted oddly with more useful books on bridge, and also curiously with Florence Nightingale's *Notes on Nursing*. Nostalgia was gracefully represented by Lady Tweedsmuir, wife of John Buchan and chatelaine of Government House, Ottawa; poetry by Charlotte Mew, who had been heartily condemned earlier by Edith Sitwell and in fact died by her own hand twenty years earlier, but was much admired by Horder. Osbert Sitwell's *Collected Stories*, with a thoughtful introduction by the novelist Francis King, found him in what was his happiest vein. 1953 produced an unusual short travel diary by the twenty-year-old journalist Tom Stacey, written immediately after his spell of National Service, and describing the life of a group of aborigines in Malaya. These unfortunates lived with the dreadful alternatives of slow extinction in the jungle, at the mercy of Chinese Communists, or refuge in a modern civilisation entirely beyond their understanding. Entitled *The Hostile Sun*, it won the John Llewellyn Rhys Prize.

Stacey still remembers Horder's curious method of entertaining authors to lunch. This consisted of a longish walk from Henrietta Street to Soho where a 'rather good' plate of smoked fish would be consumed. There would then be a move to another restaurant specialising in puddings, punctuated by occasional halts while Horder scrutinised a series of insalubrious advertisements on the notice-boards of newsagents. Few lords in fact have conducted themselves in a less lordly fashion than Lord Horder, though John Betjeman, who signed himself 'Yours sincerely, everlastingly and undoubtedly', teased him pleasantly when commending a book of memoirs by Amy Barlow, a retired school mistress. Betjeman mentioned that it had been much enjoyed by Mary, Duchess of Devonshire and commented, 'what I say is that there is nothing like the aristocracy for judging a book'. Interestingly, Miss Barlow preferred not to be designated as a teacher: 'the word is too reminiscent of the elementary schools of the past in which the pupils invariably said "Please, Teacher", "No, Teacher".' Betjeman's affection for Mervyn was not to be wondered at: it was much in line with his enthusiasm for obscure schoolmasters, unknown Edwardian architects and tea-shops in the Middlesex suburbs.

A different note was struck by the historian Cyril Falls, who had held the Chair of Military History at Oxford, and by Mervyn Horder's father, who has already been mentioned: both contributed books to the Duckworth list. Some of the catalogue descriptions about this time seem curiously naïve today. Potential readers of *Thirteen Ways to Break the Smoking Habit* were informed that 'This little book from America is much more valuable than it looks'; while Mahaschavi, 'the bespectacled Israeli chicken-farmer is quite a new type of hero in literature'; and in another novel of 1959, *Andiamo!* by John Playfair, 'Julia behaves throughout in the inconsequent manner one expects from a child of mixed British and Italian parentage'. More seriously, F.E. Halliday's various books on Shakespeare were widely hailed as throwing fresh and helpful light on the subject.

Mervyn Horder in eccentric headgear.

Mervyn's interest in music bore fruit in Mosco Carner's life of Puccini, which was triumphantly received and is still in print in a revised edition forty years on: 'No study has appeared in any language comparable to this for thoroughness and penetration, both musical and psychological', according to the chief music critic of the *Daily Telegraph*, and another leading reviewer of the day, Philip Hope-Wallace, called it 'A masterpiece ... the biography of the year in many ways, it much honours English music criticism.' At the same time, the old interest in golf was revived with books by Dai Rees, who had captained the British Ryder Cup team for several years, and on bridge by two accepted authorities, Victor Mollo and Norman Squire. By complete contrast, there was a single attempt to return to the world of theatre, with the publication of a play by Myfanwy Piper, who had recently written the libretto for Benjamin Britten's opera *The Turn of the Screw*, and was married to the leading painter and stage designer of the time, John Piper. Her play, *The Seducer*, was based on a theme of Kierkegaard, adding to the eclectic and unpredictable character of the Duckworth list. Horder was also extremely successful in selling thousands of copies of cheap school editions of Galsworthy's plays in many Commonwealth countries. The chief competition in this area came from Shaw, but not only was Galsworthy's dialogue much more natural, but Horder took trouble to see that the plays were priced more cheaply, which was a major consideration for schools in, for example, Nigeria or Sudan. The books were printed in Holland, long before it became commonplace to seek foreign printers. Horder later complained that after his departure, this advantage was lost and that there was no longer any instinct for competitive pricing.

On first acquaintance Horder could give the impression of being cranky, or even freakish, with a jarring, rather studied form of eccentricity. He could be touchy and crotchety, with a tendency towards exhibitionism, as on the occasion when he insisted on playing the piano wearing a knitted bathing dress of ancient design at a party which was, admittedly, to launch a book on knitting patterns. But there are innumerable examples of the affection in which he was held, and of his generosity to various nephews and nieces, and to others as well. He was also much in demand as a godfather: a very different type of publisher, the present reigning John Murray, and Clarissa, the daughter of John and Myfanwy Piper, who were also close friends over many years, were among those who benefited in this way. Another pleasant tribute to him came from the gifted but underestimated novelist R.C. Hutchinson, whose correspondence with the poet Martyn Skinner was edited in 1979 by Sir Rupert Hart-Davis, and includes the following story:

> Yes, I am pleased with the delightful madman who runs Duckworth's for putting *Testament* on the market again .... Moreover, on publication day, which happened to be Margaret's birthday, this enchanting lunatic and his partner in the business, an equally enchanting Viennese woman, gave us a champagne luncheon – really dry champagne! – at the Arts Theatre Club, an amusing bear-garden. Such totally unreal incidents I find *enormously* enjoyable. This man has been rewarded for his courage, for he has – this dumbfounded me – sold more than four hundred and fifty copies. Apparently there are aged booksellers in places like Uttoxeter and Lytham St. Anne's who simply cannot resist enormous books. I imagine that all the tonnage of paper is afterwards re-sold to local builders, who use it as ballast in wharfage, for the hard shoulders of motor-roads, etc.

The 'enchanting Viennese woman' was Mrs Gerti Kvergic, who was briefly a member of the board.

Later, Hutchinson mentioned Horder's reaction to his latest completed novel, *A Child Preserved,* ' "My dear fellow, how can you expect people to be interested in a book with a *Belgian* as a hero?" Maybe he had something there.' Nicholas Walker, who had briefly edited a small anarchist magazine from the Duckworth office, wrote an obituary of Horder which mentioned other characteristics, for example that he 'drove an old car or rode an old bicycle, both very carelessly. He bought cheap and nasty clothes, and cut his own hair.' But it also paid tribute to his generosity, especially to the young and poor. Ursula Vaughan Williams, the wife of the composer, was a friend for many years: they often went on holiday together, and she admired the songs that he composed. Her novel *Metamorphoses* was published by Duckworth in 1966.

The firm had made a loss in 1963 of £2,956, but this was turned into profits of £2,681 in 1964, £2,072 in 1965, and £3,710 in 1966, all of which depended on a cautious policy in writing down the value of stock. In 1967, however, there was a record loss of £4,317, which as it turned out was the signal for Horder, who was then aged fifty-five, to give up his controlling interest in the company. In the following year he transferred 9,400 of his shares in the company to Tim Simon, and the same number to Colin Haycraft.

70

THRILLS AND SPILLS
1968-1994

The new pair who now took control of Duckworth both had exceptional qualities. They were to set standards of intellectual and literary quality rarely known in the firm since the days of Edward Garnett.

Tim Simon was the son of Oliver Simon, the proprietor of a high quality printing firm, the Curwen Press, and had married the niece of Hamish ('Jamie') Hamilton, the well known publisher. In Horder's words, he was well qualified to provide both the finance and the financial wisdom to get their joint enterprise started. Very sadly, however, he was to die suddenly two years later. Had he survived, his exalted standards of book production would have been extremely difficult to sustain without further injections of cash. The reissue of Belloc's *Complete Verse*, which he designed, is a good example of his talent, one which makes many of the other Duckworth publications of this epoch look mediocre and uninspired. His obituary in *The Book Collector*, by Nicholas Barker, recorded that after starting work in the Curwen Press with his father, he had set up in 1959 a lithographic studio where artists could work 'direct onto the stone' with a handpress to produce commercial editions of prints. 'There was a real risk that print-making like this would die, only to be preserved in art colleges, but Tim with his particular combination of charm and persistence persuaded almost all the best contemporary English artists to join in the enterprise. Moore, Sutherland, Piper, Scott and Richards all worked in the studio.' Piper also illustrated an unusually well produced short book on the architecture of Venice by a fellow artist, Adrian Stokes, published by Duckworth in 1965. By the mid-sixties he had become restless. In 1966 he became managing director of the Pall Mall Press, and in 1968, with Colin Haycraft, he took control of Duckworth. In Horder's view, it was a partnership that 'promised to be one of the most exciting ventures in British publishing'. Exciting it remained, but constantly beset with financial difficulties.

Caroline Blackwood by Lucian Freud, portrait entitled 'Girl in Bed', 1952.

A much needed windfall landed when Alfred Hitchcock was looking for locations in the Covent Garden area in which to shoot scenes for his film *Frenzy*. The cast included John Finch, Billie Whitelaw, Anna Massey and Vivien Merchant. Although no record survives of the fee paid for the use of 3 Henrietta Street in the film, Horder's nephew Ted Cullinan at that time occupied the top floor with his architectural practice, and he recalls that the film paid for considerable redecoration of the Duckworth office, by then even dingier than ever. He also remembers seeing Hitchcock, installed in an open white Rolls-Royce, directing sequences from the street below. Unfortunately, although Hitchcock himself much enjoyed being photographed in action on innumerable occasions, no picture of him in the Rolls has survived. However, two stills from the film show the brass plate inscribed Gerald Duckworth & Co. Ltd on

Still from Hitchcock's Frenzy, *showing the original Duckworth brass plate.*

the railing outside the office, and the more dramatic of these, showing a film extra making a hasty exit from the office, is reproduced here. Gerald himself is alleged to have had a certain amount of stage-door life in his younger days, and his ghost may well have smiled at his office being put to this use.

The other new proprietor of the firm was Colin Haycraft, who for sheer editorial acumen was to transform the status of the Duckworth list, and for sheer financial ineptitude came very close, more than once, to sinking it beyond recovery. Horder, in spite of the temperamental and intellectual chasm between them, ranked Colin 'with the best of the strongly individualist publishers of the century'. A good collection of tributes to Colin was published soon after his death (*Colin Haycraft: Maverick Publisher*, edited by Stoddard Martin, 1995). This shines light from a variety of angles on a many-sided personality, and begins with the just observation that Colin was 'sometimes maddening, always generous, accurate, loveable and (though he would deprecate the term) quixotically *heroic*'. He was unquestionably the biggest intellect to run the company in the first century of its existence, and added to his brains was the greatest determination to seek out and publish books of the highest quality. His ambition was made a little easier by the bureaucratic conditions which prevailed at the great university presses, and their inevitable lack of his own dash and imagination. Much of the general interest which this history may have outside the ranks of those professionally involved in the book world lies in his complex character.

Colin was born in India and was only three months old

when his father was killed on active service. Later, however, having won a scholarship to Wellington, he had the luck to be taught in his last two years by an exceptional schoolmaster, Alan Ker. Clever boys and girls often derive more benefit from teaching of that quality at school than they do afterwards from dons. If Colin had not become a publisher it is possible that he might have had great influence, with his infectious enthusiasm and appetite for scholarship, as one of those rare schoolmasters of the kind that he had benefited from himself. An older friend from that time, Neville Braybrooke, has recalled Colin's comment at the age of fifteen when looking at some contemporary poems by a man named Cook. 'The chap should have been called Washer-up. The poems are nothing but the dregs of other men's sinks.' His critical faculty was clearly operating at full blast from an early age. When he went to Queen's College, Oxford, apart from winning blues at rackets, real tennis and squash, and featuring as an 'Isis Idol' in the undergraduate magazine of that name, he obtained a first in both Mods and Greats, the two parts of the classics-based degree course; and he certainly owed his academic success to native ingenuity rather than to long hours of plodding. One of his authors, A.C. Grayling, quotes in his contribution to Colin's memorial book an observation by a character in a novel by J.I.M. Stewart (himself the best kind of don). 'He was far too gifted to be a don.' That remains the verdict on Colin by many of those who knew him best.

His first and last love was for the Greek and Roman Classics, and it is worth quoting from the presidential address which he gave, in the last year of his life, to the Classical Association, in order to get an idea of his attitude.

> We should never forget that the best reason for a classical education is not so much that it 'trains the mind', as used to be so vociferously claimed by its defenders, as that it enables us to read, for their own sake, the astonishing chance remains of Greek and Latin poetry and prose. These cannot come across to us – certainly not the poetry – unless we have some knowledge of the languages. Translations are useful, and can even be good, as cribs. But who wants to be forever paddling in wellies, however green?

Colin often communicated with authors on a postcard featuring a duck upside down in a pond. Among his more inspired classical compositions were two couplets, one in Greek and one in Latin, describing the bird's posture.

πρόσθεν μὲν καὶ ὕπερθε φαιείνεται ἥλιος ἄλλοις
ἡμῖν δ' ἐνδοτέρω καὶ μετόπισθε φανείς

Which can be translated as

Some greet the sun before them and above;
But it's the kinder, hinder sun we love.

The Latin version was

Sol aliis caelo (miseris!) fulgere videtur
Nobis in caelo, Phoebe benigne, nites.

Or, in English,

Some see the sun in heaven shining clear,
We hail him shining brighter in the rear.

Above: Colin Haycraft.

Left: Hugh Lloyd-Jones with portrait bust by Marcelle Quinton.

Opposite page: Beryl Bainbridge.

'Not to know Latin,' in the words of the central character in *Joyce's Portrait of the Artist as a Young Man*, is to be 'forever a shy guest at the feast of the world's culture.'

This shows what a loss it was to the reading world that Colin never wrote a book himself. But as he observed laconically, 'Who wants a pregnant midwife?' He had come to Duckworth from being managing director, and original founding editor, of the World University Library at Weidenfeld and Nicolson, a range of eighty books published in a dozen languages. George Weidenfeld was another under-capitalised publisher with a frequent need to replenish his coffers, and on one occasion is alleged to have surprised a meeting of his board, attended by accountants and other advisers, by asking suddenly 'Does this mean I must get married again?' But at least his regular injections of cash were used to a large extent for royalties and (often excessive) advances to authors, though not to those in the World University Library, who were only offered a $3^1/_2$% royalty. One of the first to swallow this paltry bait was Richard Gregory, one of whose books for the Oxford University Press later netted him over £100,000 in royalties. As will be seen, he was in due course to become a great Duckworth star. Weidenfeld himself had a very wide experience of the book world, and his tribute to Colin as 'one of the last great humanists in British publishing' is a significant one.

After his time at Queen's College, which later made him an honorary fellow, Colin had spent two years as personal assistant to his first cousin once removed, Cecil King, the megalomaniac chief of Mirror Newspapers. King's mother was a sister of Lord Northcliffe, and King fancied that he

could repeat his uncle's rise to fame and riches and to an overwhelming influence over public affairs through the tabloid press and a range of popular magazines. Unfortunately the rise of television gradually marginalised much of the power of the press, and even though King took care that his companies made ultimately successful investments in television, his career ended in dust and ashes. Voted off the board of the Mirror Group, he ended his days in Donnybrook on the edge of Dublin. There may be some inherited connection between King's brand of arrogance and the variety of it which has sometimes been attributed to Colin. But there was a world of difference between the two. King's scorn for what he considered lesser men was grim and forbidding, and based on his craving for power. Colin's was quite different: light-hearted, almost invariably ending in a cheerful explosion of laughter which, though there were occasional exceptions, usually cancelled out anything which could have been regarded as offensive. He could certainly be scornful and dismissive of authors, agents, reviewers and other publishers whom he considered his intellectual inferiors. And there were many of them. The words which he on one occasion used about Dr. Johnson, one of his great heroes, could equally be applied to Colin himself: 'His very prejudices were always displayed with wit and educated insolence,' not least in his description of a book called *From a College Window* by A.C. Benson, the most soporific, according to Colin, in the English language: 'the river Lethe in print, whose very title is an incitement to its defenestration.' It need hardly be added that after Johnson, Gibbon was Colin's favourite English author.

But what he enjoyed most was not scoring points off his intellectual inferiors, but forming a real creative partnership with a gifted author, no matter how obscure the subject; so that what might otherwise have been an ego trip on Colin's part often turned into what might be described as an 'ego et tu' trip. Fortunately for Colin, he had left the King empire long before its decline and fall. He had taken the job there *faute de mieux*, had no talent for it and no interest in developing one. If he learnt any lessons there he soon forgot or ignored them. At Duckworth, he went on where he had left off at World University Library, but freed, or so he imagined, from the restrictions of working in other men's empires. Hugh Lloyd-Jones, Regius Professor of Greek at Oxford for nearly thirty years, and one of Colin's closest friends, observed that 'he was far more cultivated than most dons, and with it all retained a youthful gaiety and insouciance'. His great friend Richard Gregory has referred to his 'humorous aggressive courage'; as Mervyn Horder put it, 'he believed almost mystically, as well as pragmatically, in the advantages of a firm producing and distributing its own books in the heart of London, its staff working in the middle of their own book stock.'

How did he go about achieving what was, as regards literary quality, the envy of so many of his rivals? The Shakespeare scholar A.L. Rowse, four of whose books were published by Duckworth, explained that he was above all, 'like people of the first rank and quality, an *encourageur*'. Colin would have preferred a Greek or Latin term, but he would not have minded being bracketed in that respect by Rowse with T.S. Eliot, G.M. Trevelyan and Sir John Neale.

Another strong characteristic, unacceptable by the standards of today, but much less uncommon at the time, was his way of expressing his general low opinion of women; the two chief exceptions being his wife Anna, who joined the board of Duckworth in 1972, and her great friend, the immensely successful novelist, Beryl Bainbridge. Such was Colin's prejudice that it took Anna some time, and, as she puts it, 'a great deal of bullying, coaxing and insisting', to persuade him to publish Beryl. However, when *Injury Time* came out in 1977 it won praise across a spectrum which ranged from C.P. Snow to Auberon Waugh, via Martyn Goff, who hailed 'the same marvellous mixture of wit, drama and keen observation ... once again a gem'. It also carried off the Whitbread Fiction Prize for the year. How far Colin's disdain was genuine and how far a teasing pose is difficult to say, but on one occasion he described a recent illness as having been horrible but at least he now knew from direct experience what it was like to be a woman: 'one can't think, or see anything clearly.' However much or little he was teasing, it remains a fact that under Colin, women were virtually confined to the fiction list, which for many years was looked after in an inspired fashion by Anna herself – though an exception was made for Charlotte Woolf's study of lesbianism, entitled *Love Between Women.*

As we shall see, with all his mercurial qualities, Colin carried the seeds of self-defeat within him. That was his tragedy; a tragedy which sprang from a genial form of *hubris*, a contempt for his inferiors which, as in the dramas of ancient Athens, played a significant part in his downfall.

As always, Duckworth's Achilles heel was money. It has already been seen how a succession of new investors had been brought in, and in the past this had been more or less

Oliver Sacks.

successful, because the new investors, in the case of Crichton-Stuart and Horder, had on the whole been treated well, and had been reasonable people, though in the earlier case of Balston the relationship had ended in tears. When Colin took over, relations with investors seldom remained good for long.

To return to the uniquely successful side of Colin, a lucid and significant description of his powers comes from a very successful author, who, like others, became a close friend as well. Oliver Sacks was, and is, an eminent physician and psychologist whose books will be described later. But as regards Duckworth, he has explained that other publishers might have a dozen different editors, each with a particular speciality. Duckworth only had Colin, 'but Colin was so versatile, so spacious mentally, that he could grasp the central thought and intention of each of his authors, and then bring his own active powers to bear, and work on the book, work on the author, until he had achieved for it the greatest possible clarity and beauty. Such an entering-into, at once sympathetic and critical, I never felt as intrusive; I felt rather, that I had been guided to *myself*, to defining more exactly, what I needed and wanted to say.'

Few more relevant editorial tributes have been paid by a writer of consequence to his publisher. Almost more important still is a later passage: 'But beneath his playfulness, his irony, his sarcasms, his scorns, he had a passionate, defiant belief in the sanctity of the individual, and of the need, first and last, to be true to one's nature .... There was no one in the publishing world at all comparable to him, in his unremitting love of the classics, and of quality; or in his brilliance, his argumentativeness, his pigheadedness, his sweetness. Colin was never moved by profit or profitability, and intellectual and moral probity made Duckworth unique among publishers, able to maintain the highest quality in a declining, venal world.'

One of the keynotes of Colin's regime was the spirit of informality which pervaded it. Most of the authors were treated as members of the Duckworth family, all the more so after the lease of Henrietta Street was sold for £70,000 in 1971, when it still had twenty-six years to run. Since the rent there was fixed at £500 a year, any move was likely to be financially adverse in the long run. Colin characteristically brushed this aspect aside. What was far more important to him was to have an office in the same street as his house, which could spill over into it so that the house became part of the office and the office became part of the house. Several authors did much of their work in the Haycrafts' kitchen, and many brought their often serious emotional problems to Anna, sometimes arriving for lunch and staying till the next day. Frequent publication parties were held, with packers from the warehouse chatting away happily to classical scholars, who in any other context were remote and detached figures, and to the novelists who were nurtured by Anna. With the help of Janet Boud, she managed to do all the catering, whether for two or a hundred, at a fraction of what would otherwise have been the cost. The fact that the rent of The Old Piano Factory, which was the name of the new premises, was £3,000 a year, to be increased in 1979 to £5,750, with another review to be held at the end of a further seven years, was a minor matter, at least in Colin's eyes, though Horder strongly disapproved of the move.

On the death of Tim Simon, Colin acquired from his widow the shares which he had owned in the company, adding them to the those which he had acquired from Horder in October 1968, and thus gaining complete overall control. He could therefore do as he pleased, anyway for the time being, and what pleased him very much was the new situation described above. A leading Hampstead bookseller, Ian Norrie, has a happy memory of calling at The Old Piano Factory to collect his weekly order,

> entering up the fire escape and into the general warehouse-office. Beryl Bainbridge was sitting scribbling away, Mervyn was reading, close to a piano. A packer was packing, Colin was looking learned as always. He glared at me by way of greeting – he didn't care for me. I said, 'Give us a tune, Mervyn.' Mervyn leaped to the piano, Beryl joined him and they played and sang a Victorian ballad. Publishing was fun then.

No other publisher in England, perhaps in the world, conducted its business in this way. When, in 1991, the firm moved to premises in Hoxton Square, to the north of Liverpool Street Station, the new building had the advantage of being able to contain the entire stock of books with space available for more, as will be seen. But it plainly changed the way Colin had operated during those informal years in Camden Town.

Where did the books come from? Most general trade publishers depend largely on agents for the supply of new and even old authors. Few agents were prepared to deal with Colin, in view of the trifling advances offered, and the worse than dilatory treatment of royalties. Colin's attitude to them was cheerfully robust: 'Those who can, write. Those who can't become publishers. If they fail as publishers they become agents. If they fail as agents, Heaven help them.' It is part of his claim to fame that he nevertheless not only found authors himself, but authors of books of an extremely high standard, several of which he himself played a large part in creating. He was lucky in that most of these authors not only had decently paid academic jobs, but would have had great difficulty in getting their work published elsewhere, and this often (but not always) compensated for slender and unpunctual financial rewards.

The affection in which these authors held Colin, and their gratitude for the endless trouble he would take with them editorially, is brought out by the tributes they paid him in Stoddard Martin's composite portrait mentioned above, which is indispensable for any perception of the nature of the firm under his rule. Pride of place among these should perhaps go to Oliver Sacks, whose tribute to Colin has already been quoted, and who followed up his first book, *Migraine* (published by Faber & Faber), with an exceptional series of case studies of sleeping sickness and Parkinson's Disease, entitled *Awakenings*. First published in 1973, it was born of one of the most fruitful partnerships between publisher and author that Colin was responsible for, and also gave Harold Pinter the idea for his play *A Kind of Alaska*. The book consisted of a study of various varieties of mental and physical disturbance which Sacks had helped to treat at the Albert Einstein College of Medicine and as Consultant Neurologist to the Little Sisters of the Poor, and elsewhere in New York. It won the Hawthornden Prize, was chosen by no less than five *Observer* critics as a Book of the Year, and was hailed by W.H. Auden as 'a masterpiece'. It

Beryl Bainbridge at the party given to celebrate the reissue of Three Weeks *by Elinor Glyn, serenaded by Joe Wong.*

was followed in 1986 by the weirdly titled *The Man Who Mistook his Wife for a Hat*, which was described by Anthony Storr, doyen of contemporary British writers on psychology, as 'equally enthralling: no higher praise is possible'. It explores a wide range of perceptual and intellectual aberrations, showing a profound sympathy which enabled first the author and then his readers to enter the patients' world. In his preface to the revised paperback edition of *Awakenings* in 1982, Sacks paid special tribute to Auden, as a mentor and friend who had 'awakened' him, and this edition was dedicated to the memory of Auden and of A.R. Luria. A well-known critic of the day, A. Alvarez, commented that 'Dr. Sacks writes beautifully and with exceptional subtlety and penetration into both the state of mind of his patients and the nature of illness in general', while another reviewer put it 'in the fine tradition of the very best medical literature, where the writer-doctor reports what his patients have taught him, as well as what he has tried to do for them'.

In the wake of these books, and in the same field, came *Pride and A Daily Marathon* by Jonathan Cole, describing the achievement of a patient who had been struck down at the age of 19 by a rare neurological illness depriving him of all sensation below the neck. Confined at first to a wheelchair, though he later learned to walk, he somehow developed 'elaborate tricks and strategies to control his movements, enabling him to cope not only with the day-to-day problems of living, but with the challenges of work, love and marriage'. Sacks, in a foreword, described the book as 'an attempt to articulate, through the experience of a rare and exceptional patient (and his equally exceptional doctor) a situation beyond imagining'.

This group of books in the field of neurology provided enlightenment and sometimes comfort for families and other carers coping with the victims of appalling handicaps, who until comparatively recent years had usually been abandoned to their fate. This strand in the very varied tapestry of the list is one of which Duckworth can be extremely proud, and has led to other later developments, also of great value, in the wider field of general psychology.

In 1973 an effort was made to produce a less dingy catalogue than usual to mark the firm's 75th birthday. It contains a potted history which listed, besides those mentioned earlier in this book, the novelist Elizabeth Goudge, the journalist Godfrey Winn, and the delightful American comic poet Ogden Nash. Finally it mentions that the entire staff, including packers, numbered only about a dozen, and boasts that it is one of the few publishers to have been 'controlled throughout its history by editors who have employed accountants, rather than *vice versa*'. If they were few then, they are far fewer now, yet Duckworth could still truthfully make the same claim today.

In this catalogue Beryl Bainbridge's second novel, *The Dressmaker*, was praised to the skies by reviewers. 'A formidable talent, a writer to her nerve ends', and 'Like the better Hitchcock films Miss Bainbridge suggests a claustrophobic horror all the more poignant for the brilliantly etched domestic setting.' There were many more comments in the same vein. Not for the last time, the author was short-listed for the Booker Prize. She had drawn on the Liverpool background which, as it happened, she had shared in early youth with Anna Haycraft, now firmly installed as Duckworth's fiction editor, and about to blossom as a novelist herself. For a time, Bainbridge helped with publicity and sales in the office, and indeed was often sent off by Colin to remote corners of England to promote a variety of Duckworth books. She has played a huge part in the success of the firm from that time right up to the present, yet she too was abominably treated when it came to royalties. Jane Conway-Gordon, who worked for Colin for two years from 1975, recalls Beryl anxiously approaching the formidable accounts manager for a small payment, from a large total long overdue, in order to buy a much needed pair of shoes. Lamentable though this sort of treatment was, many authors who had other earnings felt compensated by the quality of the editorial inspiration and help that they received, and also by the unique family atmosphere in the firm, and stuck it out with Duckworth when they could very well have gone elsewhere.

Another of Anna's stable of writers was Caroline Blackwood, the great-niece of Belloc's inspired illustrator, B.T.B., who remained a close friend till her death in New York in 1996, Anna having spent much of the last month at her bedside. It is hard to describe her unique vision (which was more successfully expressed in short stories than full-length novels) but it was based, in Anna's words, on 'a kind of appalled wit which never fails to illuminate the realities'. She had married, first, the painter Lucien Freud, and last, the great American poet Robert Lowell.

Blackwood's books for Duckworth were *For All That I Found There*, *The Stepdaughter* and the macabre *Great Granny Webster*, which was short-listed for the Booker Prize. However, she was one of those who eventually had such a row with Colin that in spite of her collaboration and close friendship with Anna, she moved to another publisher. Another brilliant and much acclaimed novelist, though of a very different type, was Penelope Fitzgerald. Having published two excellent novels, *The Golden Child* and *The Bookshop*, with Duckworth, she too moved on to another firm more reliable in the matter of royalties. She proceeded to win the Booker Prize with her next novel, and later the Heywood Hill prize for her whole oeuvre. But it was new writing of this quality that inspired the literary editor of the *Guardian*, Bill Webb, to salute Duckworth's as the best fiction list in London.

Delving back into the past, Duckworth also brought out at this time a six-hundred-page collection of stories and poems by the ill-starred American, Dorothy Parker, doomed to a life of double martinis and deep romantic disappointment, but with an extraordinary ear for human speech, a rare gift for irony and a tenderness for lost and unrequited love, all expressed with a wonderful sense of form. Anna Haycraft had by this time begun her own very successful writing career. Her motives were twofold. First was the urgent need to add to the small salary which Colin took as managing director. To this end she began what was to become a wonderful column on 'Home Life' in the *Spectator*, balancing the rather monotonous but immensely popular 'Low Life' of Jeffrey Bernard and the equally unedifying 'High Life' of Taki.

It is difficult to select an example of these short pieces, which could be described as the Catholic housewife's answer to Dorothy Parker. A dozen others are just as good, but the following has the advantage of bringing in two of Duckworth's other idiosyncratic stars.

Sometimes Beryl laughs so much she has to lie down. She did the other day. We were in our local trying to have a talk without disturbance – something impossible in the home – and a foreign gentleman apparently mistook me for a lady of the night. I can't imagine why. I was wearing my ladylike grey flannel and had my hair scraped right back. Nonetheless he kept telling me that he had just 15 minutes and more or less insisting that I nip outside and help him to occupy them. I told him I was a married lady and very religious and he got quite indignant. He would tap himself on the chest saying he had all the love, and then he'd attempt to do the same thing to me, saying I had the experience. Sauce. It was at that point that Beryl had to lie down, sobbing with uncontrollable hysteria. I was trying to maintain a serious demeanour because I didn't particularly want to hurt the wretched man's feelings, and also these scenes can get quite tense if one is not careful. Fortunately the 15 minutes elapsed and he was required back at his place of work.

We took Jeff to Mass last Sunday, creeping into the pub beforehand for a fortifying vodka. What was my astonishment – for this is far from Jeff's manor – to hear a voice saying 'Hi Jeff.' 'Hallo Boris,' responded Jeffrey with what seemed to me to be modified enthusiasm. Boris bought us all a drink and insisted on lending Jeff a fiver, so I said as we departed, 'What a nice man', and Jeffrey agreed that he was charming but added that he had a nasty job. 'Oh poor thing,' we said sympathetically, 'what does he do?' 'He's a burglar,' said Jeff.

That's one of the things I like about this part of the world – you meet all sorts. Only last week I was trotting towards the station averting the eyes from the winos who stand or sit by the back wall of the cinema, a line of pee leading from each to the gutter, reminding one of the chickens and chalk lines, when a young man darted out of a doorway requesting the loan of a match. No point here in pretending not to have seen him, so we got into conversation. He had two companions – one utterly silent, and one a pretty girl. He said they were Irish travelling people and I didn't like to ask what that meant – gypsies, tinkers, or just Irish people who got about a lot? With the novelist's interest in raw material I enquired their names. He said reassuringly that he was known as Jerry the Street Fighter. So I hastily asked the name of the girl.

'Mary de Rothschild,' she responded.

'Pardon?' I said.

'Mary the Lost Child,' she repeated. That made me want to cry, so I departed the poorer by a match and a couple of quid. Jerry offered me a swig from his bottle and I said I was a teetotaller. He intimated that it might be nice if they all came home with me, and then he kissed me. I really must change my perfume. When I *think* of the strictures I put upon the daughter about not talking to strangers.

A couple of years ago I broke Rule Number One. I had been to see Caroline and instead of calling a cab to the house I went off to pick one up at Brompton Road. Unfortunately the pubs were just emptying and every time I hailed a taxi it was whipped away by pairs of very alarming men, some bold in black leather hung about with chains, and some with Mexican-type moustaches. I was not disposed to argue with them so I stood in the rain growing quietly desperate. After a while a private car drew up and a gentleman leaned out and asked if he could give me a lift. Before you could say 'rape' I had hopped in. Can you believe it? I realised immediately, of course, that I was a much more foolish person than I had previously supposed and began a very Cheltenham tea-table conversation about the weather and the cost of private education in my most modulated tones. He was a dear kind man up from the country for the day and he drove me straight home – some considerable distance – declining to come in and meet my husband and join us in a cup of coffee. I don't know what he must have thought. *No* well brought up woman gets into the cars of strange men. I was lucky there, but I have instructed my friends never to let me out alone after a convivial evening. I can't be trusted.

The *Daily Mail* described one of the four collected volumes of Anna's 'Home Life' pieces, all published by Duckworth, as 'as English as Jane Austen (a tribute all the more remarkable since Anna is half Welsh and half Finnish) and as fortifying as a glass of vintage brandy'.

Here is her besotted American publisher on the subject of her first novel (Alice Thomas Ellis is Anna's *nom de plume*):

> In the pages of *The Sin Eater*, which I'd eventually tracked down through a London shop that was helping me collect the books of the *Spectator* fraternity, I heard 'Home Life' echoing in the sharp-tongued dialogue, the biting wit, the keen-eyed and economical delineation of a family's psychological and emotional in-fighting. But in the novel I unexpectedly found that the kitchen door

Above: Anna Haycraft (Alice Thomas Ellis).

Left: Michael Dummett.

of Ellis's social comedy opens on the timeless: in her fiction the here-and-now unfolds in the presence of the last things – death and judgement, heaven and hell. As Rose says during her final robust excoriation of the changes that in recent years have rendered the Catholic Church unrecognizable to her, 'They've forgotten all about eternity'; in *The Sin Eater* I discovered that Alice Thomas Ellis's unique gift as a novelist is her ability to make us remember.

In this context it is interesting to note what the author herself had to say about how she came to write her first novel. 'I was so annoyed,' Ellis confessed, 'that ... I stirred out of my habitual indolence and wrote a book called *The Sin Eater*. I put it in the form of a novel, since books give better scope for ungoverned rage than more sober works and I had to do something rather than sink into despair.'

Rose, the central figure of the novel, put her finger on the trouble as follows:

> The last time I went to Mass – and it *was* the last time – there was the [parish priest] facing the congregation, standing behind his table and joining in the singing of the negro spirituals and the pop songs and Shall-we-gather-at-the-river. There has always been a hint of catering about the Mass, but previously the priest had the dignity of a master chef busying himself with his *specialité*. Now he seems like a singing waiter in charge of an inadequate buffet. One is tempted to stroll up and ask for a double martini and enquire who on earth forgot to put the doings on the canapés.

Of the few voices raised in protest at these changes, Anna's became at once the most eloquent and the most fearless. Critical acclaim for her novels grew steadily. The four published between 1980 and 1985 – *Birds of the Air, The Twenty-Seventh Kingdom, The Other Side of the Fire* and *Unexplained Laughter*, earned, respectively, the following comments from reviewers: 'A minor classic' (*Sunday Times*); 'A painfully brilliant comedy' (*New York Magazine*)'; 'One of the brightest and most original of contemporary novelists' (Alan Massie); and 'Every page gives pleasure' (Harriet Waugh).

It is worth noting that the Duckworth list in the 1970s and 80s was by no means restricted to fiction at one end and academic books at the other. In 1975 Duckworth reissued the book which had first brought Evelyn Waugh onto their list, his biography of Rossetti. In the interview quoted earlier, he had dismissed it as hurried and bad, adding 'I haven't let them reprint it.' After his death, however, his executors decided otherwise. And in 1977 Colin brought out a topical book on *Skateboarding*, at the suggestion of his son William. Published at the height of the craze, it sold no fewer than 85,000 copies.

1978 was particularly rich in biographies. Subjects included such diverse figures as Danton, Syrie Maugham (the controversial interior decorator wife of Somerset Maugham), Mary Webb, and Captain Bligh, of Mutiny on the Bounty fame. On a more scholarly note, Dacre Balsdon's *Romans and Aliens* was described by Philip Toynbee, at that time the *Observer*'s leading non-fiction reviewer, as 'the most enjoyable work of history I have read for a long time.' Michael Dummett, the newly appointed Wykeham Professor of Logic at Oxford, produced *Truth and Other Enigmas*, and Sir Kenneth Dover, President of Corpus Christi College and also of the British Academy, published his treatise on *Greek Homosexuality*. Two years later, another Professor, of Jurisprudence this time, Ronald Dworkin, produced a book which was even more widely discussed in much wider circles, *Taking Rights Seriously*. These books are all evidence of Colin's ability to swoop down on the high tables of Oxford and carry off works of great distinction, often helping to inspire their composition himself. It should be stressed – and it is perhaps the greatest feather in Duckworth's cap in this period – that his intellectual equipment for operating in this rarefied field was probably unique in the field of publishing.

Other less exalted non-fiction books that made a stir about this time included *Feed your Face*, by Dian Buchman, described as 'a herbal guide to natural beauty and health', a book so ecologically correct that it was reprinted no less than eight times, and sold 57,000 copies, though taken on largely by chance. On a quieter note, there was also a return to agriculture, one of the areas in which the firm had been successful in its earliest days. *The Wheat Plant*, by John Percival, originally published in 1921, was reissued in a new editon in 1974, with a handsome jacket designed, like others about this time, by David Gentleman. M.L. Ryder's majestic study, *Sheep and Man*, ran to 846 pages and was priced at £55, which one would have thought would have put it out of the reach of all but the most single-minded shepherds. Heath Agnew's *History of Hereford Cattle* and Gill and Vear's *Agricultural Botany* became standard textbooks, as, in its bizarre way, did Eva Crane's *The Archaeology of Beekeeping*. Other favourite subjects from the past cropped up again in *Lieder Line by Line* by Lois Phillips and, back at the bridge table, Norman Squire's *Theory of Bidding* and *Squeeze Play Simplified.*

Another important book was *The British Conquest and Domination of India* by a very distinguished retired Indian Civil Servant, Sir Penderel Moon. Although he made a large financial contribution to its publication, it was published at £60, in one volume of 1,232 pages. This was a very unhappy piece of publishing, for the text actually falls neatly into two halves, with Part 1 ending at the time of the Mutiny, and it should obviously have been brought out in two volumes, or as two separate books. However, Duckworth calculated that the subsidy was insufficient for that purpose. The result was a book which was too expensive to buy, and, if bought, too heavy and inconvenient to hold.

Another book by a distinguished and unusual public servant was published in 1993, the year before Colin's death. *Great Game, Grand Game* was the title of the memoirs of Tom Rogers, who had first served as a Political Agent with the new-born government of Pakistan at the time of the large-scale butchery which followed Partition. He continued to lead a more adventurous existence than most diplomats, and had various crises to defuse – one in Buenos Aires when an Argentine pilot landed in the Falklands, and another in Ottawa when De Gaulle roused the French separatists in Quebec. Later, on the author's first day as Ambassador in Bogota, the England football captain Bobby Moore was jailed for alleged theft a week before a World Cup match, in a country where suspects are locked up as guilty until proved innocent, sometimes many years later. In the same year there was also published a somewhat optimistic history of Ghana, a country also slightly known to Colin from the time of his brief stint working in Nigeria for Cecil King. The author, John Carmichael, had the unusual distinction of having been made Honorary Chief of Warriors of the Fete Tribal District, while his father had been Honorary Chieftain in another region of Ghana. These two last authors revived the long tradition of bizarre adventures in remote countries, started long before by Cunninghame Graham, and continued on the Duckworth list by Evelyn Waugh, Robert Byron and Tom Stacey.

In 1981, thanks to Hugh Lloyd-Jones who served as joint editor, Duckworth brought out one of the most prestigious books of its day, both academically and for its value to the amateur with an interest in the subject. *History and Imagination* was a collection of essays by the colleagues and friends of Hugh Trevor-Roper, on his retirement as Regius Professor of History at Oxford. Far from being a remote occupant of an ivory tower, Trevor-Roper was known not only for his scholarly books on the seventeenth century, with later excursions into other periods, but also for his unfailingly lively, sometimes somewhat tart articles and reviews in the *Sunday Times* and later elsewhere, and for television appearances and other public comments on anything connected with the Second World War (in which he had done important work for MI5). His early book, *The Last Days of Hitler*, had been a well deserved best-seller, he had outshone his friendly rival A.J.P Taylor and was the only Oxford professor – as opposed to administrator – to have been made a life peer. He was also given a supreme accolade when Colin described him as 'Gibbon *redivivus*', come to life again. This delightful book begins with Trevor-Roper's own inaugural lecture as Regius Professor in 1957, and ends with his valediction in 1980. The contributors included several of the most famous and also readable historians of the day. The great Fernand Braudel wrote on the 'The Rejection of the Reformation in France', and Professor Dimitri Obolensky on 'The Varangian-Russian Controvesy'. The Jameson Raid was the subject chosen by Robert Blake, who was a former fellow Censor of Christ Church with Trevor-Roper, and whose daughter Deborah was later to become a director of Duckworth. Michael Howard, another old Christ Church colleague, contributed a fascinating analysis of 'Empire, Race and War in pre-1914 Britain'; Richard Cobb, later Professor of Modern History, one of whose own astonishing books was published by Duckworth, wrote a piece entitled 'Thermidor or the Retreat from Fantasy'. There were also more specialised essays, less accessible perhaps to the casual reader, but rich in scholarship, by G.R. Elton, Arnoldo Momigliano and Valerie Pearl, the President of New Hall, Cambridge. Lloyd-Jones commented that while it could not represent all its hero's historical interests, the collection gave an indication of their range.

It was Trevor-Roper's obvious relish for his subject, and his insistence on the part played in it by imagination if it was to remain alive, that had inspired him to be so generous with time and encouragement as a tutor, and had helped to give his lectures such brilliance for the benefit of wider audiences. Lloyd-Jones was right in stating that 'few living authors have a more felicitous ear for the rhythms of the language'. This is particularly evident in his own two lectures, which are not only a real joy to read, but which inspire his readers to think for themselves. He ended his farewell lecture with the charming story of his having, long before, crossed swords vigorously with Evelyn Waugh. At the end of the battle, Waugh, scenting victory, had written in the *New Statesman* (on 2 January 1954): 'One honourable course is open to Mr. Trevor-Roper. He should change his name and seek a livelihood at Cambridge.' Although not at all in the way that Waugh had had in mind a quarter of a century earlier, this had indeed come to pass when Trevor-Roper became Lord Dacre of Glanton and Master of Peterhouse, Cambridge. Altogether, it is difficult to think of a book that does Duckworth more credit on a wider front, or one that is at once so enlightening and so entertaining.

To turn to philosophy, Alasdair Macintyre's study in moral theory, *After Virtue*, first published in 1981 and revised and added to in 1985, had an exceptional reception not only from his fellow professionals but also from readers. As well as exploring the connection between philosophy and history, and the relation of moral philosophy to theology, he explained his conclusion (reached in the years before and immediately after the fall of the iron curtain and the collapse of the Soviet Union) that the moral defects and failures of Marxism arise from the extent to which it embodies the ethos of the modern and modernising world and that nothing less than a rejection of a large part of that ethos will provide us with a rationally and morally defensible standpoint from which to judge and act. A fellow philosopher, Stephen Lukes, described *After Virtue* as 'unquestionably one of the most lively, interesting and provocative books to have appeared for at least a decade'. The book includes the delightful epigram, 'All power tends to co-opt; absolute power co-opts absolutely.'

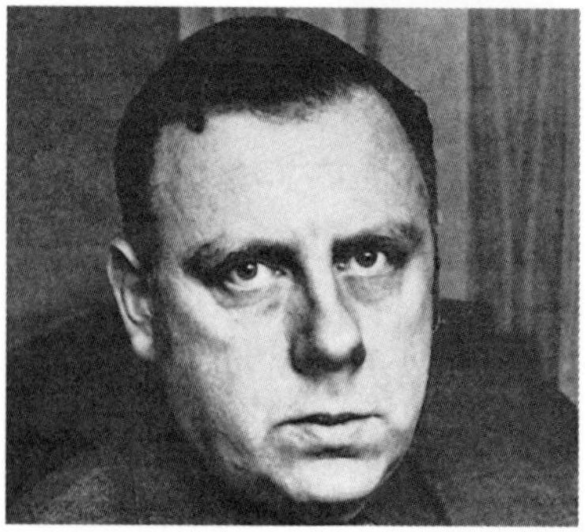

Above: Jeffrey Bernard.

Left: Alasdair MacIntyre.

Attention was also paid to a different field. In the section of the catalogue categorised as 'Cookery, Health, Self-Help' is to be found Tina Hobin's *Belly Dancing: for health and relaxation* (1982), rather surprisingly for those who had previously regarded it as a form of entertainment. Colin celebrated it by giving a particularly hilarious publication party, introducing the rather unexotically named belly dancer herself with the words, 'And now, for your umbilical delight, we present Miss Tina Hobin.' Her gyrations have never faded from the memory of those lucky enough to have been present, and 12,000 copies of the book were sold.

In a very different vein was Jeffrey Bernard's *Low Life*, like Anna's *Home Life* books a collection of pieces that originally appeared in his *Spectator* column. The column recorded his slow but sure disintegration under the effects (chiefly) of vodka and cigarettes, though throughout the last decade of his life his friends and foes alike never ceased to marvel at his powers of survival. Odder even than any other aspect of Bernard's existence was the way in which he retained the affection of those who had suffered from him, in word and deed, in a very wide variety of ways. In his book, among other relics from a past for which 'chequered' is the grossest of under-statements, the author reproduced a friendly letter from the editor of the *Daily Mirror*, Mike Molloy, in answer to a request for details of the author's career there – forgotten by him but certainly not by anyone else concerned:

> On a certain evening in 1969 you rang my mother to inform her that you were going to murder her only son. If you would like further information, I can put you in

touch with many people who have enjoyed similar bizarre experiences in your company.

Anna continued to befriend Bernard, right down to his dying day.

Confirming the infinitely wide range of subject matter that commended itself to Duckworth is a book of a more staid character, *Early Croatian Architecture* by Vladimir Goss, an appealing work in spite of the abysmal quality of the illustrations. Still in the Balkans (though not illustrated at all) was *The Vlachs* by T.J. Winnifrith, which includes the memorable sentence 'There are not many Vlachs at Pisodherion.' Nearer home was *East End 1888* by W.J. Fishman, Professor of Political Studies at Queen Mary College, with an eloquent introduction by Richard Cobb, a book which gives a chilling picture of the life of the London poor exactly a hundred years earlier. These desperate scenes were also the setting for *The Ripper and the Royals* by Melvyn Fairclough, published in 1991. The interest of this book goes far beyond the serial murder of prostitutes, since it claims that Prince Edward, Duke of Clarence, the eldest son of Edward VII, had secretly married a Roman Catholic commoner called Annie Crook, and by her had had a daughter, Alice. What is beyond doubt is that this Alice, whoever she was, later had a son by the celebrated painter Walter Sickert, through whom the basis of this extraordinary (and of course unproved) story reached the author.

On a more comic note, the popular political journalist Alan Watkins produced a hilarious account of a libel action in which, after twenty-five years as a columnist, he had recently been involved. The plaintiff was a well known Labour MP and Shadow Minister, Michael Meacher, who sued for words used in the *Observer* no less than four years earlier. Watkins had written that Meacher liked to claim that his father had been an agricultural labourer, whereas in fact he was an accountant. Watkins also wrote about the resignation from the party of a former Labour MP, Eric Moonman, as a result of an intrusive questionnaire dispatched by Meacher to Health Authority chairmen. Perhaps unkindly, Watkins compared Meacher and Moonman to the louse and the flea celebrated by Dr. Johnson. By the time of the trial, which lasted nearly three weeks, this jest had long been forgotten. Meacher lost, becoming the first libel plaintiff in over fifty cases to lose to a journalist. Another unusual, perhaps unique feature of the case was that a politician was suing a political journalist who was himself a qualified barrister. Altogether, the case made a big contribution to what could still be called, at a pinch, the gaiety of the nation. Watkins later followed this up with *A Conservative Coup*, an account of the fall of Margaret Thatcher published only a year after the event.

In the mid-1980s there was a departure into a very different field. A series of paperbacks on home computers and their use was originated in 1983 under the control of Ray Davies, Duckworth's production director. Initially, the series was a great success, filling a gap in a vast emerging market. For a year or two all went swimmingly: for example, *Using the Commodore 64*, published in October 1983, quickly sold 25,000 copies. Most of the early titles in the series were instant successes, reprinting as soon as they were published. Granada was the only other UK publisher to be involved in home computer books in the first two years, but in 1985 many other publishers typically joined the expanding market, which by December 1986 had reached saturation level and was in decline. Many of the small retailers that had sprung up to service a hungry public disappeared and the glut of computer books that remained were destined for remainder merchants or pulp mills. The speed with which the turnaround took place was unprecedented and resulted in a substantial loss to Duckworth. Whether or not this could have been predicted remains a matter of opinion.

The sheer range of all these titles, from an exalted level of scholarship right down to the lower depths of the world of Jeffrey Bernard, is evidence of the range of Colin's perceptions, enthusiasms and sympathies. 'From Aristotle to Belly Dancing' just about sums it up. Deborah Blake, who had joined the firm in 1978 and became a director in 1988, had the formidable task of seeing ninety per cent of the entire list through the press. Colin had no other editorial help, but spent a great proportion of his time working on manuscripts, encouraging authors, helping them to develop their ideas and to move forward when they got stuck, as authors often do, and restraining them when they raced ahead too fast. This was the work at which he excelled, and his appetite for it was insatiable. But it may also have provided a form of escape from the aspect of publishing which he neglected, namely the practical side of running a business.

In 1988 he had to face the fact that Duckworth was in severe financial difficulties. At a time of high interest rates the company had run up a large overdraft with no prospect of being able to reduce it in the foreseeable future, and was on the verge of trading illegally. Colin was forced to start 'looking for a millionaire'. The search bore fruit in September 1988, when an exotic figure decided to make a substantial investment in the company.

Roger Shashoua's origins were in Lebanon, and his career had been remarkable. Basically an inventor, he had come to head the largest patent licensing group in America, and was involved in a whole range of business ventures in Europe, Africa, the Middle East, Japan and China. He had almost succeeded in establishing a major Chinese trade and cultural city in the Docklands area of London, 'for the benefit of young scientists and inventors'. He became a visiting professor and honorary fellow of a number of universities in Britain, China and Korea, and he and his wife both joined the Duckworth board to protect their investment in the company. Quite how Colin came across the Shashouas is uncertain, but ambitious though short-lived plans were formed to found new companies under the Duckworth umbrella, and to widen the range of operations. Roger Shashoua also wrote an autobiography describing various aspects of his own financial wizardry called *The Paper Millionaire*, which Colin published. The honeymoon period with Colin was brief, however, and by the summer of 1990 the Shashouas were as eager to depart as Colin was to replace them with a new shareholder. Before they left, Colin made virtually his only mistake in over-paying, for a book by a popular celebrity. An advance of £30,000 was given for an autobiography by Ernie Wise, the partner of Eric Morecambe in what was in its time the most famous comedy programme ever shown on television in Britain. Of the print-run of 10,000, less than 2,000 were sold. This was an uncharacteristic lapse on Colin's part, never repeated.

The Shashouas' shares were then acquired by an aspiring fiction-writer named Michael Estorick, whose father had made a great collection of twentieth-century paintings, including works by Derain, Braque and Picasso. But what made it unique was the quantity and quality of works by the Italian Futurists which it also contained. Marinetti and Gino Severini are the two most familiar names among them, but others like Balla, Boccioni and Campigli are no less rewarding, though a great deal less well known, along with the sculptors Manzu and Marini. All these works had been bought with great skill at a time when very few people were interested in them, and many of them had cost next to nothing, anyway by comparison to their later values. Four years after Eric Estorick's death in 1993, his son opened a gallery at 19a Canonbury Square, where these works, of a kind which can rarely be seen elsewhere in England, can be admired in congenial surroundings.

Michael Estorick's acquisition of the Shashouas' shares in Duckworth did not of course solve the shortage of working capital in the firm. However, hope now sprang from an unexpected quarter. Professor Trevor Smith (later made a life peer), the Chairman of the Trustees of the Joseph Rowntree Reform Trust, approached Colin with the information that the Trust was seeking to make a new investment in the publishing sector. Rowntree had for some years owned a share in Gollancz, and in view of the Trust's charter, which included the object of making investments that 'benefited reform and freedom of speech', this had been appropriate since the first of these aims had been central to Victor Gollancz's own philosophy, and his list contained many books devoted to them. The Rowntree directors of Gollancz had then enabled Livia Gollancz, who controlled the firm on the death of her father, to sell it to Houghton Mifflin in America for a much higher price than she had been on the point of accepting from another potential buyer. Rowntree had thus made a considerable profit on their original investment.

The Duckworth list was, however, a very different affair: for example, the twenty pages of their list of books in print in 1987 contains only six books on politics and world affairs and eight on social studies, including the quaintly named *Tearoom Trade: A Study of Homosexual Encounters in Public Places,* published in 1970. However, Smith later claimed that it was not with any thought of getting books taken on that supported their own objectives that Rowntree made their investment, but, altruistically, because they considered it desirable that a small independent firm like Duckworth should survive when so many others had disappeared. The Rowntree directors, all being well, would later enjoy the kudos of at least playing a part, perhaps a leading part, in running a prestigious company. It was all a wonderful example of the academic institutional mind fancying itself in the field of commerce – and, to be fair, they had done well enough out of Gollancz. However, the Rowntree directors seemed unaware of Colin's methods before stepping in. Whatever the need for fresh money, and however soon, and often, he needed to be saved from his saviours, he never came to have any intention of modifying his method of running the company, which was based on having his own way on most matters, and all too often letting both pounds and pennies look after themselves, with the inevitable result that there was a chronic shortage of both. This was something that it may have been hard for an investor in the firm to spot before becoming involved in the day-to-day business of the company, and the failure to do so led to hideous problems.

Smith himself was soon to be appointed Vice-Chancellor of the University of Coleraine in Northern Ireland, and David Shutt, the other director nominated to the Duckworth board by Rowntree, was preparing to stand unsuccessfully as a Liberal Democrat candidate for parliament in Yorkshire. Yet even before this their relations with Colin had become extremely strained, since neither in temperament nor approach had they anything in common.

The omens were therefore unfavourable from the start, and it seems strange that Rowntree should have invested £538,750 in such an inappropriate firm, representing 26% of the Ordinary Shares and 100,000 newly created preference shares. Estorick owned 191,250 of the Ordinary Shares as against Colin's 169,800, but Colin had a crucial option to buy out Estorick within a period of eighteen months from the date of Estorick's investment in the company (that is to say by 29 March 1992) which gave him potential protection, always assuming that he could find the money, against the possibility of their falling out.

It was in 1990, after Estorick had made his investment and during the negotiations with Rowntree, that Colin sought the advice of one of the few Duckworth authors who was also a qualified chartered accountant, specialising in venture capital. Stephen Hill had worked with the well known firm of Binder Hamlyn for seven years, as well as in industry, when he decided at the age of thirty-three to enrol as a mature student at King's College, London to study the classics. (One of the small companies which he had helped

Beryl Bainbridge with Stephen Hill.

on its way was Godfrey Cave, a remainder and reprint house which was later sold to Penguin.)

Hill was subsequently the co-editor of *Dhatu Patha: the Roots of Language*, an academic work which linked the linguistic roots of Greek and Latin words with Sanskrit. It was published in 1991, and when the London Library commented to Duckworth that it was incomprehensible, Hill spent two months writing *Concordia: The Roots of European Thought*, indicating how the roots of language worked by a comparative study of Vedic and Greek philosophy. Hill was now to become instrumental not only in saving Colin and his family from ruin, but in putting Duckworth on the road to considerable financial success. In the early days of their investment, the Rowntree directors recognised Hill's business capacity and asked that he should be invited to participate in board meetings with a view to finalising reporting procedures and delegation of authority, in other words to see that the company was run in a businesslike fashion and not in accordance with Colin's unpredictable whims. On 23 October 1990 the Board thanked Hill for his handling of the issue of new shares and drawing up the subscription agreement which was signed by all the shareholders. They added that there was no further general scope for his involvement, but that he would be consulted as and when issues might arise which would make it useful.

Estorick had already had a novel published by Duckworth in 1986 entitled, ironically as it turned out, *Can't Buy Me Love*. His object was to be in charge of fiction at the firm, for which he was to be paid a salary of £10,000 a year. Colin had verbally agreed to this, and Estorick was installed. Very soon, however, Colin and Anna decided that Estorick was unsuited to the task. It must be said, however, that Estorick had the flair to spot a novel which Duckworth took on after it had been turned down flat by seventeen other firms. *The Tap Dancer* by Andrew Barrow went on to win the coveted Hawthornden Prize and also the McKittrick Prize, awarded for a first novel by an author over the age of forty. The book had excellent reviews and is still in print in paperback, with Picador.

To put it mildly, the situation became uneasy. The Rowntree directors claimed that it was immoral of Colin to have accepted Estorick's money 'on the false basis that he would teach him how to be a fiction editor', and had then made no attempt to do so. Against this, it was claimed at Duckworth that Estorick had failed to turn up at meetings on time and then complained that they had started without him. It was really a question of oil and water not mixing. But on top of all this internal strife, within a few months, Duckworth's business was hit by two problems, one of them expected, the other a bolt from the blue.

First came the outbreak of the Gulf War in January 1991, which led to a severe slump, lasting about six months, in retail sales of all kinds, books not excepted. Like other publishers, Duckworth suffered their highest ever returns of books from the shops. Secondly, the lease on The Old Piano Factory was due to expire at the end of 1992, and alternative accommodation for the office and warehouse was essential. This was found at 48 Hoxton Square, near Old Street Station, on the northern fringes of the City, though Hill was not pleased when it transpired that the money which he had raised to be used as working capital for Duckworth's everyday publishing activities had largely been spent on this acquisition of a freehold building, when all that was required was a rented office. However, it was in an area designated for commercial redevelopment, and there was a good chance, later realised, of its being a good investment. The business suffered heavily during the period of the move, since apart from the office and staff, 270,000 books had to be physically moved. The disruption lasted for about six weeks, since much of the physical labour was carried out by the executives and staff.

In September 1990 a Business Plan had been prepared for the benefit of the Rowntree directors, and with some resistance from Colin. ('What is a Business Plan? I just publish books, and get on with it. The only equipment you need in this business is an india rubber and a waste-paper basket.') While preparing this plan, Stephen Hill felt that he was beginning to understand Colin's quixotic approach to company organisation and finance, which he decided was roughly on the following lines. Marketing was completely unnecessary, since customers would be led to the books by their sheer quality, which would also inspire them to pay exceptionally high prices for them. Contemporary authors in general were paid excessive advances and royalties, and it was better to stick as far as possible to authors who had been dead for two thousand years. Wisely, overheads were stringently controlled, but a rather expensive in-house distribution system was maintained, so that the staff could see and handle the books, and send out review copies quickly. Interest payable to banks was an abomination, and interfering investors did not deserve dividends, and should be replaced at frequent intervals. The success of the firm's finances was to be judged by whether the salaries were paid, regardless of the true source of the funds used. Hill realised that all this had to be changed without Colin's involvement, and preferably without his knowledge, while his attention was concentrated where it should be, that is to say on editorial matters, and on the cajoling of literary editors.

As we have seen, the Business Plan was prepared in the autumn of 1990 and there immediately followed a complete change in the economic climate, so that the results predicted for the first half of 1991 were in no way achievable. The Rowntree directors were not unreasonably determined to take measures to improve matters, and a decision was taken in April 1991 by the controlling votes of Rowntree and Estorick to commission an outside report on the day-to-day running of the company from Jack Angell, a director of an entirely different type of publishing company based at Newton Abbott in Devon, where the Duckworth sales director, Henry Russell, had previously worked. The report made various criticisms and recommendations, but on the whole Colin considered that Angell had no understanding of how he, Colin, intended to go on running the company, and airily dismissed his conclusions. However, in May 1991, Hill drew Colin's attention to a unique opportunity for expansion which was entirely in line with his scholarly preoccupations. The bookshop chain Chapter & Verse had gone into receivership, and as a result of cross-guarantees with the publishing firm of Bristol Classical Press in respect of bank borrowings, the assets of the latter were available for purchase. This plan was greatly to the advantage of Duckworth, since not only would the acquisition make an excellent fit editorially in view of Duckworth's existing backlist, but the Duckworth warehouse could easily accommodate the extra stock and turnover. It was also a vital step, as otherwise there would have been no commercial justification for finding the money with which to buy out Estorick. The proposal initially found little favour with Estorick or the Rowntree directors, but after a day-long board meeting, Hill finally persuaded them that the acquisition was commercially essential.

Having drafted the offer letter for Colin to have typed and to sign, Hill then went to America on other business. A week later, he telephoned Colin to check that the transaction had been completed, only to learn that Colin had not heard from the Receiver. On telephoning the Receiver himself, Hill discovered that only one offer had been received (and accepted), not from Duckworth but from a rival firm. Further inquiry revealed that Duckworth's offer was still sitting in Colin's out-tray. Hill increased Duckworth's offer by £10,000 to £122,000, and mercifully it was accepted. The entire stock of 110,000 books belonging to BCP (as it is called for short) was moved into Hoxton Square, and the two businesses were amalgamated. Colin celebrated by composing the following couplet for the 1991/2 catalogue:

Bristoliense Classicum fuit Prelum:
bene est quod anate iam renascitur dignum.

The Bristol Press is dead: what luck
Tis born again now worth a duck.

Relations between the two factions were almost as bad as could be, and at a board meeting on 26 November 1991 Estorick is minuted as having thrown a file at Colin and

Colin Haycraft at home, photographed by Beryl Bainbridge. As his favourite English author Gibbon expressed it, 'Two causes, the abbreviation of time, and the failure of hope, will always tinge with a browner shade the meaning of life.'

then having left the room in anger. The nadir was reached in early 1992, when Colin was actually sacked as managing director. He was locked out of his office, the locks were changed and he was only reinstated after informing Estorick's solicitors that he intended to exercise his option to buy Estorick's shares, payment for which would only become due eighteen months later, and which was finally made, with Hill's help, at the eleventh hour.

All this imposed a considerable strain on the executive directors and the staff, and above all on Colin, who suffered a mild stroke on the very day when he succeeded in buying back Estorick's shares, 7 December 1992, a day ominously described by one of the lawyers involved as 'a life shortening experience'. Indeed, it turned out to be a prelude to the much more severe stroke that was to carry him off two years later. The boardroom battles certainly did not help his health, but his own personal financial problems with capital gains tax owed on the sale of his shares to Roger Shashoua several years earlier placed, if possible, an even worse strain on him in the last year of his life.

It may also be asked what caused the war in the first place. Sadly, the answer can only lie in Colin's frequent refusal to be bound by the most elementary rules of commercial common sense, and to his ever-optimistic determination to run Duckworth as a private fief, for the enjoyment and fulfilment of himself, his employees, and his devoted authors. Despite all these vicissitudes, he had not lost his editorial flair. It took a new direction when he began to bring out a series of collections of the sayings of great authors. These were of uniform length, 64 pages, and sold at £4.95. An auspicious start was made with Oscar Wilde, of which 83,000 copies have been sold to date. Colin himself edited the Dr Johnson volume, and others in the series included Byron, Churchill, Dorothy Parker, Sydney Smith and Trollope.

But almost the last book that he took on was in an entirely different genre from anything that Duckworth had published before. *Major Major* was a family history by the then Prime Minister's elder brother, Terry Major-Ball. Terry received a certain amount of editorial help from a journalist, James Hughes-Onslow, who later had the pleasure of being told by the Prime Minister, 'You are almost one of the family now.' Colin took a great deal of pleasure in the publication of the book.

On the other hand, Colin was still an inspired publisher of academic books, not least in the all important matter of pre-selling substantial numbers of bound copies to American university presses, chiefly those of Harvard and Cornell. However, he only once went to America, and in later years never attended the Frankfurt Book Fair. His chief hero in the ancient world was the poet Horace, but his devotion to Gibbon, already mentioned, eclipsed all the others. And one might well apply to Colin the words used of Gibbon himself by his greatest friend and benefactor, Lord Sheffield: 'He united, in the happiest manner imaginable, two characters which are not often found in the same person, the profound scholar and the peculiarly agreeable companion.'

On the departure of Estorick, the Rowntree directors were in a minority and ceased to have anything to do with the day-to-day running of the company. The acrimonious board meetings came to an end, and the staff were at last able to concentrate on their jobs. In consequence, and with the help of Bristol Classical Press, profits rose to £79,592 in 1993 and £118,899 in 1994.

On Colin's death of a stroke on 24 September 1994, the Rowntree directors pointed out that the dividend on their preference shares had not been paid, and claimed further that the company was not in a position to do so. Then, five days before Christmas, they called an Extraordinary General Meeting of the company with a notice to wind it up voluntarily, and to appoint liquidators. This would have been disastrous for Duckworth, and came as a terrible blow to Colin's bereaved family, but after some difficulties Stephen Hill succeeded in persuading the Rowntree directors to sell their shares to funds under Hill's advice. On Christmas Eve he was able to tell Anna, in triumph, that she had nothing to worry about. The decks were finally clear, and business resumed. At first it was business as usual, but before long it would become something a great deal better.

Colin and Anna Haycraft and supporters on the day in 1992 when Colin regained control of Duckworth.

Duckworth's new premises at 61 Frith Street, by Lucinda Rogers.

DUCKWORTH ARISES
1995-98

Colin's death was a terrible shock for all concerned. But something had to be done, quickly, in order to preserve the excellent momentum which had been built up over the past two years Happily, 1994 had been a very successful year. Each month had seen a record in sales figures, empty champagne bottles were regularly to be seen in the dustbins at Hoxton Square, and whatever his personal financial troubles, Colin had the satisfaction of seeing the company making great progress in the last few months of his life.

The problem of succession was acute. He had however given the matter some thought, since he had already suffered a minor stroke and was moreover approaching the normal age for retirement. His own preferred candidate, Robin Baird-Smith, who had spent the previous ten years as editorial director of Constable, another independent company of comparable size, was duly appointed in March 1995. Stephen Hill, who became Chairman of the company on the departure of the Rowntree directors, welcomed Baird-Smith aboard with a formula which was unusual even by Duckworth standards. Tongue firmly in cheek, he informed him that 'You are three things that I disapprove of. You're a Catholic. You're a Wykehamist. And you're a Socialist. You've got the job.' Efforts were even made to merge Constable with Duckworth, but it proved impossible to agree terms. However, Baird-Smith lost no time in achieving vital results, first by fending off various vultures who were seeking to carry off the firm's better known authors, on the grounds that their personal loyalty to Colin now no longer applied, and that they would be far better off with a firm that actually paid their royalties, and even offered decent advances. It was particularly important to cement relations with Beryl Bainbridge, who had been no better treated financially than anyone else. She had already acquired an agent (much to Colin's dismay) and her departure would have been a major disaster for Duckworth, but her retention, with the help of a three-book contract with Abacus, was the first of Baird-Smith's coups. Meanwhile, Deborah Blake had come to take responsibility for Duckworth's academic books.

Secondly came the setting-up of a new list devoted to naval and maritime history. This came about because the editors at the successful firm Conway Maritime Press had become dissatisfied with their owners, the military publishing house of Brassey's. Robert Gardiner and Julian Mannering were approached by Duckworth, and the resulting new imprint, Chatham Publishing, brought out its first books in July 1996 and has gone from strength to strength. The first title, *Nelson's Favourite,* written appropriately enough by a descendant of Anthony Deane, Samuel Pepys' favourite shipwright, was an auspicious start, selling well in a Book Club edition and, in co-edition form, to the Naval Institute Press in Annapolis, Maryland, as well as successfully in the home trade. The Naval Institute Press have been loyal supporters of the Chatham list and have published some 80 per cent of their titles in the United States. A book launch was held in the Great Cabin of HMS *Victory*, hosted by the Second Sea Lord Sir Michael Boyce; and the setting, in Nelson's old quarters, with a light summer breeze coming in off the sea, marked a happy beginning for the list.

Since then the imprint has grown quickly and by the summer of 1998 had some forty-five titles in print representing a broad range of maritime interests – the Nelsonic navy, so beloved of the readers of Forester and Patrick O'Brian; the navies of the two world wars; nautical archaeology; local and traditional craft; and ship modelling. Britain is no longer a dominant maritime nation but there is still a great demand for books and information on her seafaring past and the interest is truly international – Nelson is as great a hero in the Far East as in Britain and Chatham's books find their readers in every corner of the world. Some are sold by direct mail, others to specialist bookshops, and the books may be found as easily in a maritime museum in Madrid or Mystic Seaport in Connecticut as in the National Museum in Greenwich. Authors include academics as well as popular historians and enthusiasts; some had been previously published by Conway Maritime Press. This resulted in an action brought by Brassey's which was successfully defended. One-book authors mix with such prolific names as Dudley Pope, while Nelson himself appears in print in the seven-volume *Dispatches and Letters of Lord Nelson*, first published in 1846 and now reprinted in paperback.

The philosophy of the editors is to publish useful and original reference books with high production standards which will appeal to serious historians as well as to enthusiasts. They are history books and do not concern themselves with defence matters or yachting, though, on the naval side, the historical context of the present-day Royal Navy is a significant theme. The imprint shares with Duckworth the intention to be the best in its chosen field. It is a model of how a business should expand, and although nothing specific is at present in view, it has encouraged those responsible for Duckworth to keep a sharp eye out for future opportunities of a parallel kind.

Another very different field in which Baird-Smith's own interests and expertise continue to bear fruit is that of psychology and its place both in medicine and sociology, all areas in which Duckworth had been publishing books of distinction for many years, going back even beyond the days of Oliver Sacks and Richard Gregory. In 1997 Duckworth launched an important new series in conjunction with the Tavistock Clinic, to make available the clinical and theoretical work being carried out there, and to improve the understanding and treatment of psychological disturbances at all ages, at both an individual and also a family level.

Opportunities for further expansion will no doubt be found in due course, not in a silly 'dash for growth', but on a well calculated, unhurried commercial basis. Baird-Smith explained his standpoint in an interesting article in *Concord*, a quarterly publication of the English Speaking Union, where he spelled out the way in which a small firm could prosper, in contrast to the failure of other larger organisations which are driven by formulas devised by 'accountants unfamiliar with the world of real books'. In larger firms – and he mentioned Collins, where he had worked between 1979 and 1985 – the crucial relationship between author and editor was nowadays all too often ignored. 'It is the editor', he wrote, 'who should batter the sales force ... who should sparkle at the sales conference and persuade the men and women of the road to put every ounce of their energy into making the author's book a success.' He added that the editor should be freely available to the author on the telephone, and should never be 'in a meeting' if it can be avoided. Baird-Smith's methods are not the only ones that are effective, but for Duckworth they have certainly led to some impressive successes. He also pointed out that an energetic small firm can often 'nip in like Sir Francis Drake with really good small scale marketing strategies while the armada of huge galleons lose their sense of direction and founder'. Dame Muriel Spark, whom he had acquired for Constable, was a case in point. Her previous publisher had been gobbled up not once but twice, and she had decided to move somewhere where her editor was always there to talk to her, 'and did not communicate through the means of a spewed-out inaccurate computer print-out'. The proof of the pudding had been in the bookshops: Constable had quadrupled her sales.

Baird-Smith also insisted on a long overdue improvement of the standards of book design, as this volume itself bears witness. Unlike his original partner Tim Simon, Colin had not been interested in making his books look good, and the necessary money was certainly not there to do so. (An exception to this was the design work of David Gentleman on some of the jackets, and indeed on the Duckworth duck.) For Colin, the intellectual content of the books was the be all and end all, and virtually all Duckworth books had been indistinguishable from each other for the past thirty years. Another huge improvement was the introduction of attractive catalogues, actually using laminated covers in full colour, instead of the dingy stock lists which had appeared year after year ever since the 'utility' requirements laid down in 1940. Ray Davies, whose time at Duckworth goes back to 1966, two years before Colin's arrival on the scene, recalls that at that time the invoices were all written out by hand, and the sales department possessed only a single typewriter, on which the lever for moving to a new line was broken. But since it was the only one, it could never be sent away for repair. There had also been a venerable armchair, with a broken leg, propped up by some long forgotten typescript, whose author remained patiently unaware of the useful purpose which it was serving. Hoxton Square, too, was a spartan establishment. But an exciting move to more central premises in Frith Street, Soho, was made two months before this history was published.

Apart from these thoroughly satisfactory developments, there was a third area in which Duckworth took the lead, in an independent fashion and resolutely opposing the accepted wisdom of the day. This was nothing less than the great debate about federalism in Europe, the Treaty of Maastricht and the threat of a common currency. A whole series of loosely connected books was published by Duckworth, which may well turn out to be, in practical terms, an unusually influential programme. A crucial factor was that these books appeared not on an unknown list but over the imprint of a firm with impeccable intellectual standards, carefully nurtured over many years under Colin. No Duckworth book could be written off as being lightweight or ill thought out, even by those who disagreed with the conclusions drawn by the various authors from the evidence which, selectively or otherwise, they had assembled.

The first shot was fired by William Cash, M.P. for Stafford, Chairman of the Conservative Backbench Committee on Foreign Affairs and member of the Select Committee on European Legislation. His message could be summarised as 'Yes to European co-operation, No to European federalism' and he spelt out the details in a 128-page paperback, *Against a Federal Europe*, published in November 1991. Apart from its initial impact it has found its way into university libraries all over the world, and seven years later, when Jacques Delors had disappeared and Chancellor Kohl appeared to be tottering, the author still receives thoughtful inquiries from readers far and wide. Cash followed this up the following year with a 62-page paperback called *Europe, the Crunch*. Colin's interest in politics did not go much beyond the world of Aristotle, but Duckworth went on to publish a symposium book edited by Stephen Hill and entitled *Visions of Europe*, which included contributions from the former Prime Minister Margaret Thatcher, the former chairman of the Conservative Party Norman Tebbit, the current President of the French Assembly Philippe Séguin and the Munich lawyer Dr Manfred Brunner, who at the time was taking the German government to the Karlsrühe Constitutional Court on the grounds that the Treaty of Maastricht breached the German constitution over the issues of sovereignty and the abolition of the Deutschmark. The book, which covered the whole gamut of issues from economics, law and defence to federalism and sovereignty, became the first Euro-realist bible and was co-published in Germany, France and Spain. Another important title was *Sovereign Britain* by Norman Lamont, a former Chancellor of the Exchequer, which concentrated briskly on the main issues.

There was a far wider readership for *Castle of Lies* by Christopher Booker, an analysis of the iniquitous regulations imposed on this country by unelected authorities in Brussels. Supported by a particularly enterprising sales campaign, it has so far sold over 12,000 copies. To give one example from many, it was especially effective in savaging the scandalous Community Fisheries Policy, which has resulted in the dumping of hundreds of thousands of tons of dead fish back in the sea every year, and has had an appalling effect on fish stocks. Sir William Nicoll, who had served as Director-General of the Council of Ministers from 1982 to 1991, commended the authors for exposing 'some of the nonsenses of drafting and enforcement', but reproached them for their belief in conspiracies among 'mad officials'. There can be no doubting the central message of the book, that many lives and businesses are being ruined by European Law, and quite a few, as Quentin Davies M.P. pointed out in a review, by Whitehall; for example in the Department of the Environment, which added so many further rules to the EU Directive that it was a hundred times the length of the original EU version. Booker and North are following this up with *Scared to Death*, an equally ambitious analysis of the bogus science and media hysteria behind the succession of food scares which have been such a feature of British life since the 1988 salmonella crisis, culminating in the unprecedented catastrophe inflicted on British agriculture by BSE in 1996.

Another very different book, written by Booker alone, was *A Looking Glass Tragedy* (1997). Originally turned down by another publisher for fear of libel writs, it was welcomed by Baird-Smith as an unusual contribution to modern history, dealing as it did with 'how and why people get history wrong'. Its theme was the heated controversy over the handing over of 70,000 Cossacks by the British Army to the Communists in 1945, a procedure which filled many of those who had to execute it, or who witnessed it, with horror and disgust. An ill-supported conspiracy theory was developed thirty years later which finally led to the farcical Tolstoy–Aldington libel case in 1989. The book had mixed reviews, but warm tributes were paid to it by several experts on military history, including Sir Geoffrey Cox, Sir David Hunt and the Marquess of Anglesey.

To return to the world of fiction, 1996 also saw Beryl Bainbridge's greatest triumph so far, and yet again she was short-listed for the Booker Prize. *Every Man for Himself* is set on the fatal voyage of the *Titanic*, and the fascination of the story rests not only on the range of characters, some of them dubious, others merely over-confident, but also on the structure of the ship itself, with its ballrooms and billiard-rooms, its swimming-pools and its chapel, and the social stratification of the whole enormous enterprise. Every detail was carefully researched, yet nothing weighs the story down or hinders the action. Not surprisingly, but quite unusually for a novel of great literary artistry, it sold 22,000 copies in hardback, and over 100,000 in paperback. Quite by chance, its publication preceded yet another film on the subject, and by a richly deserved stroke of luck its publication in America gave the quite false impression that it was merely the book of the film. It therefore sold far better there than it would have done on its own, far superior, merits. The author then turned her attention to the subject of the Crimean War, and the novel that ensued, *Master Georgie*, published in April 1998, is already receiving more coverage than ever.

In the run-up to the centenary year, the classical tradition was further maintained by *Ancient Greek France*, a comprehensive study by A. Trevor Hodge, Professor of Classics at Carleton University, Ottawa; sourcebooks on *The Jews Among the Greeks and Romans* and *Greek Medicine*; and biographies of Philip of Macedon and Alexander the Great by Nicholas Hammond, Emeritus Professor of Greek at Bristol. Thus the classical torch burns as brightly as ever at Duckworth. It is fuelled partly by the steady sales from the ever-growing backlist, which now includes *Learn Latin* by Peter Jones, originally based on a course serialised in the *Daily Telegraph*, and which has now sold 17,000 copies in paperback. This part of the list is also constantly being added to by younger scholars who are naturally attracted to the firm. This strong general revival of classical studies, just at the time when they were coming to be considered out of date and 'irrelevant', is a reassuring sign for the culture of the country, and Duckworth can be proud of its major role in feeding it. They have Colin and his devoted scholar friends to thank for it.

Other sublimely independent spirits who added lustre to the list towards the end of the period covered by this history include two more controversial professors in the best Haycraft tradition. John Vincent, Professor of History at Bristol, and Roger Scruton, formerly Professor of Aesthetics at Birkbeck College, London, both gave glorious offence to those who had been duped by the wilder absurdities of political correctness. Vincent wrote the first book in a well devised series of Intelligent Person's Guides, covering the philosophy and evolution of history, and his sequel on women in the twentieth century is eagerly awaited. Among other material, it will contain much evidence that the Suffragette Movement, contrary to popular myth, played only a minor part in the attainment of votes for women in 1922. Of great interest are Vincent's comments on what attracts authors to the list, and keeps them there: '... the Duckworth qualities of backing a hunch, taking decisions quickly (no ponderous succession of outside readers!) lively promotion (I found myself with a fan club in Australia) ... Production was faultless, and speedy: any second thoughts about misplaced commas were dealt with by my wonderfully intelligent copy editior. From first to last, my experience has convinced me that a small organisation based on personal contact will always beat a giant bureaucracy from the author's point of view.' It would surely be impossible to ask for a warmer tribute.

Roger Scruton, whose first book in the series dealt with philosophy, is following up with *An Intelligent Person's Guide to Modern Culture*, which will point out that the term is widely abused by journalists to cover every kind of collective habit, including those of 'pop' and 'youth'. He argues for the religious origin of culture and defends 'high culture' against radical and deconstructionist critics. The book may with all modesty be described as 'a must for all people who are fed up to their tightly clenched front teeth with Derrida, Foucault, Oasis, Richard Rogers and the late Princess Di'.

In a different but not incompatible field, a new development has been announced under the inspiration of a significant figure from the world of *Esquire* and Hollywood. Stephen Hill has invited Tom Hedley to create a series of 'Duckworth Literary Entertainments', some of which will have film associations, and others may find homes on publisher's lists in America. The series is still in embryonic state at the time of writing, but the fact that one of the first projects concerns an anthropological analysis of The New America and its folk by a descendant of Darwin – no less – is a stimulating opening shot.

It is not inappropriate that after so many crises, with tragedy more than once so narrowly averted, this history of Duckworth should end on a comic note as well as a successful one. If eccentricity has been an occasional feature of the Duckworth world for many years, one of its highlights appeared early on in the drawings of Heath Robinson, whose name had indeed passed into the language at an early stage in his career. H.G. Wells recognised his genius back in 1914, when he wrote: 'I have been ill and frightfully bored and the one thing I have wanted is a big album of your absurd beautiful drawings .... You give me a particular pleasure of the mind like nothing else in the world.' Duckworth published two of his collections of anti-German war cartoons in 1915 and 1916. His comedy was quite free from scorn or malice; he was simply content to ridicule the antics of the real world, but in a manner which needed to be straightfaced to have its maximum impact. He worked for many serious manufacturing companies, and it was indeed his sheer seriousness as an artist that was the key to his genius. As he put it, 'At the slightest hint that the artist himself was amused, the delicate fabric of humour would fade away.' In the 1970s Duckworth reissued, with Mervyn Horder as editor, seven collections of his best work, several of which were still in print twenty years later. In 1997 *Railway Ribaldry* was reissued in smart new covers, followed shortly afterwards by *Inventions*, of which 'Safety First Cricket', composed half a century before cricketers began to dress up as if for ice hockey or garage work, is a fine example.

Much has been said about the diversity of the Duckworth list, and the skill and discipline with which it is now controlled. Taking all these factors into account, and with the appointments of the post-Haycraft period so well settled in, the firm seems set to go on improving its position, as far as general management and policy are concerned. The more observant literary agents have already taken note of this, and now eagerly approach Duckworth when they would never have dreamed of doing so before. Colin's editorial flair would have been hard for anyone else to match, but so much that was wrong in other ways has now been firmly and, one imagines, permanently put right that Duckworth can now surely embark on its second century of activity with confidence in continued development and success.

Thanks ultimately to Stephen Hill's remarkable salvage operation, but for all the other reasons already given, including what has been described as 'the triumph of the editorial voice over the accountant's spreadsheet', a new Golden Age may well be dawning. What is certain is that the management is far more clearly focussed and better equipped to face the future than it was on that happy day when Gerald Duckworth first hung up his brass plate in Henrietta Street, a hundred years ago.

Safety First Cricket

'Safety First Cricket' from Inventions *by W. Heath Robinson.*

Virginia Woolf Beryl Bainbridge Simone de Beauvoir Hilaire Belloc Jeffrey Bernard Caroline Blackwood Quen
Crisp R.B. Cunninghame Graham Charles Doughty Roland Firbank John Galsworthy Elinor Glyn Maxim G
D.H. Lawrence W.Heath Robinson Oliver Sacks Edith Sitwell Tom Hedley Virginia Woolf Beryl Bainbridge Si
de Beauvoir Hilaire Belloc Jeffrey Bernard Caroline Blackwood Quentin Crisp R.B. Cunninghame Gra
Charles Doughty Roland Firbank John Galsworthy Elinor Glyn Edith Sitwell Maxim Gorky D.H. Lawre
W.Heath Robinson Oliver Sacks Tom Hedley Virginia Woolf Beryl Bainbridge Simone de Beauvoir Hilaire Be
Jeffrey Bernard Caroline Blackwood Quentin Crisp R.B. Cunninghame Graham Charles Doughty Ro
Firbank John Galsworthy Elinor Glyn Maxim Gorky D.H. Lawrence W.Heath Robinson Oliver Sacks Edith Si
Tom Hedley Virginia Woolf Beryl Bainbridge Simone de Beauvoir Hilaire Belloc Jeffrey Bernard Caro
Blackwood Quentin Crisp R.B. Cunninghame Graham Charles Doughty Roland Firbank John Galswor
Elinor Glyn Maxim Gorky D.H. Lawrence W.Heath Robinson Oliver Sacks Tom HedleyVirginia Woolf B
Bainbridge Simone de Beauvoir Edith Sitwell Hilaire Belloc Jeffrey Bernard Caroline Blackwood Quentin Cr
R.B. Cunninghame Graham Charles Doughty Roland Firbank John Galsworthy Elinor Glyn Maxim Gorky I
Lawrence W.Heath Robinson Oliver Sacks Edith Sitwell Tom Hedley Virginia Woolf Beryl Bainbridge Simon
Beauvoir Hilaire Belloc Jeffrey Bernard Caroline Blackwood Quentin Crisp R.B. Cunninghame Gra
Charles Doughty Roland Firbank John Galsworthy Elinor Glyn Maxim Gorky D.H. Lawrence W.Heath Robin
Oliver Sacks Edith Sitwell Tom Hedley Virginia Woolf Beryl Bainbridge Simone de Beauvoir Hilaire Belloc Jef
Bernard Caroline Blackwood Quentin Crisp R.B. Cunninghame Graham Charles Doughty Roland Firl
John Galsworthy Elinor Glyn Maxim Gorky D.H. Lawrence W.Heath Robinson Oliver Sacks Edith Sitwell T
Hedley Virginia Woolf Beryl Bainbridge Simone de Beauvoir Hilaire Belloc Jeffrey Bernard Caroline Blackw
Quentin Crisp R.B. Cunninghame Graham Charles Doughty Roland Firbank John Galsworthy Elinor G
Maxim Gorky D.H. Lawrence W.Heath Robinson Oliver Sacks Edith Sitwell Tom Hedley Virginia Woolf B
Bainbridge Simone de Beauvoir Hilaire Belloc Jeffrey Bernard Caroline Blackwood Quentin Crisp I
Cunninghame Graham Charles Doughty Roland Firbank John Galsworthy Elinor Glyn Maxim Gorky I
Lawrence W.Heath Robinson Oliver Sacks Edith Sitwell Tom Hedley Virginia Woolf Jeffrey Bernard B
Bainbridge Simone de Beauvoir Hilaire Belloc Jeffrey Bernard Caroline Blackwood Quentin Crisp R.B. Hil
Belloc Jeffrey Bernard Caroline Blackwood Roland Firbank Quentin Crisp Edith Sitwell R.B. Cunningha
Graham Charls Sacks Hilaire Belloc W.Heath Robinson Cunninghame Graham Charles Doughty Oliver Sa